Profitable Consumer Lending

A Guide To
Lending, Collection
and
Compliance

Robert D. Hall
F. Blake Cloonen

Bankers Publishing Company
Boston

Bankers Lending Series

Library of Congress Cataloging in Publication Data

Hall, Robert D., 1927–
 Profitable consumer lending.

 (Bankers lending series)
 Includes index.
 1. Consumer credit—United States.   2. Collecting of accounts—United States.   I. Cloonen, F. Blake.
II. Title.   III. Series.
HG3756.U54H34   1984   332.1′753′0685   84-319
ISBN 0-87267-047-3

Executive Editor: Robert M. Roen
Production Editor: Nancy Long Coleman
Cover Design: William Samatis

We wish to thank the Credit Union League of Massachusetts for all the help they gave in supplying forms and reviewing the material, and Mr. Robert Podrat, President, who was especially helpful and cooperative.

Contents

About The Authors

Robert D. Hall, Jr. is President of Corpex (East) Inc., Boston, an international financial advisory service. Before joining Corpex he was Chief Executive Officer of St. Jean's Credit Union and prior to that he was Vice President and Director of Marketing at Charlestown Savings Bank in Boston.

Mr. Hall is the author of the book, GETTING READY FOR NOW ACCOUNTS and has published articles in Bank Marketing Magazine and Financial Marketing Magazine. He has also written articles for Business Week and Industry Magazine.

He has been a member of the Credit Union Executives Society, the Public Relations Society of America, Bank Marketing Association, Savings Institutions Marketing Society of America, and the New England Bank Marketing Association.

Mr. Hall holds a B.A. from Brown University and has completed graduate work at Boston University. He has also attended The School of Management sponsored by the Savings Bank Association of Massachusetts.

F. Blake Cloonen, principal of CLOONEN ASSOCIATES, is a graduate of Boston University, the Graduate School of Savings Banking at Brown University, and the Savings Banks Senior Management Development School at the University of Massachusetts. He has extensive experience as a manager and consultant in the fields of lending and collections.

Mr. Cloonen served on the original Technical Committee of the Mutual Institutions National Transfer System, Inc., for the National Association of Mutual Savings Banks. His current banking affiliations include membership in the Savings Banks Association of Massachusetts, serving on the Consumer Loan Committee for over ten years; the Greater Boston Consumer Credit Association, Inc., serving as President (1968–1969), Vice President (1967), and Director (1963–1970); and the New England Association of Credit Executives, Inc., serving as Chairman of the Bank Relations Committee.

Preface

Nothing is perfect. There is always room for improvement in every person and in every procedure. The credit system on which the American economy depends is no exception. This book focuses precisely on ways and means of improving the specialized consumer credit granting, lending, and collection methods and procedures already quite familiar—in whole or in part—to most retail credit organizations whether they are banks, credit unions, savings and loan associations, finance companies, department stores, oil companies, or retail credit granters.

Since their inception, business establishments and lending institutions have used credit to increase their profitability and to finance their growth. In the decades following America's great Depression, consumer credit has become a pervasive force in our capitalistic society. With the return of the veterans of World War II and their desire to create a better life than they and their parents had known before the War, credit for every man became the commonplace means of buying "the good things of life." Rather than debt being the stigma it had been in the past, it became the accepted norm as America moved into the second half of the Twentieth Century.

As our nation's exploding population soared into the 1950s, the Americans' life style changed radically. Those too young to remember the Depression were unhindered by practical knowledge of the economic hard times experienced by their parents. The new "easy credit"—without stigma or concern for the consequences—created the means for people to realize their financial goals. By the millions Americans obtained advanced educations and purchased homes through government loans, financed appliances, automobiles, vacation trips, and luxuries undreamed of by their parents through the easy credit extended by merchants and the quick capital available from lenders anxious to keep money flowing out into the economic mainstream.

The burgeoning demand of the American people for more and more goods and services has been met by the Nation's retailers and financial institutions which have expanded their businesses over the years by extending more and more credit. The result is a country that is dependent on credit. The statistics are staggering. In 1960, the total consumer debt in the United States was $56 billion. Ten years later, by 1970, that amount had doubled to $112 billion. By 1980, it had nearly tripled to $330 billion. And, estimates are that by 1990 America's consumer debt will exceed $500 billion, a ten-fold increase in just 30 years! Combined with mortgage debt and corporate indebtedness, the total outstanding credit in the United States exceeds the Gross National Product. Credit has become the fuel of our economy during the second half of the Twentieth Century.

While the enormous growth of credit has fueled the United States' economy, it has also created some formidable challenges for those who extend the credit. Heading the list is the need to institute lending and collection techniques that will result in a profitable turnover of funds. One of the major problems facing today's lenders and credit granters is the growing number of consumer defaults and bankruptcies. Unless consumer credit can be extended and serviced at a profit to the creditor, the ready availability of funds to lend to consumers will dry up and economic decline will set in.

This book brings together many lending and collecting techniques—plus some new ideas and methods—which have been observed and used in scores of financial institutions and retail establishments. The key to successful credit granting and collecting lies in the skillfull use of all the available knowledge and experience accumulated through the years from proficient and successful lenders and collectors in all types of businesses. What has worked successfully for a small loan company can work equally well for a large savings and loan association; an innovative technique developed by a collection attorney can be put to use by a retailer's collection department; a credit union's credit-review criteria can be applied to a credit-card issuer's review techniques. If financial institutions, department stores, and other credit grantors put into practice the majority of the suggestions contained in this book, there will be little need for their concern about the "bottom line." The application of the proved principles and procedures for granting credit and collecting accounts will produce profits for the creditors who apply and follow them.

On the following pages readers will find the secrets (which are mostly common sense) of successfully lending money, extending credit, and collecting past-due accounts and will learn how to apply these strategies to their own operations. This book has been written to help creditors increase the probability of developing a sound basis for each procedure they choose to use. Another advantage of this book is that it deals with practical (not theoretical) techniques. Every one of the things discussed have been practiced under field conditions and proved in actual use by all types of creditors.

Turning the credit department into a money-making factory will not be the result of good luck; it will be the result of careful forethought and planning before implementing credit policies that are sufficiently flexible to fit today's economic gyrations; establishing office procedures appropriate to one's business and marketplace; and setting in place manual and automated systems by which the entire credit and collection process will operate smoothly and efficiently.

That is what this book is all about: credit policies, procedures, and systems, a compendium of useful information about extending credit and collecting past due payments. While some of the material may be familiar to you, much of it will be new. You should pick and choose, selecting those ideas most suited to your operations. Every creditor can profit through the knowledge of more efficient methods of granting credit, lending money, and collecting consumer loans. If you learn just a few of the lessons included in these pages and incorporate them into your operations, our labors in writing this book will have been worthwhile.

1

Establishing a Retail Lending and Collection Facility

PLAYING THE CONSUMER CREDIT GAME

In years past, the different types of credit-granting and money-lending institutions confined themselves to a "limited-loan playing field." Commercial banks were concerned with commercial loans, savings and loan associations concentrated on real estate loans, mutual savings banks offered savings-secured loans, credit unions made the majority of auto loans, finance companies made unsecured consumer loans, and retailers extended both secured and unsecured credit only to purchasers of their merchandise.

Today, the consumer credit industry has laid out a "level playing field" for itself and loans of all types are being offered to the general public by every type of lender—including major retailers, brokerage firms, mutual funds, and insurance companies. For the first time in history, many creditors are becoming full-service lenders. Money and credit terms are being offered to any credit-worthy individual or entity for any worthwhile purpose because usury ceilings, for the most part, have been raised or erased. Now the return on funds invested for a short term into loans of all types can be greater and far safer than from almost any other type of investment. But, the newcomers to the field of general consumer credit are encountering the same problems that are well known to the old-timers in the consumer credit game: training personnel, taking applications, complying with laws, keeping records, billing, collecting, and skip tracing.

AN INNOVATIVE BANKER

Ben was an imaginative and innovative banker. He was light years ahead of his conservative competitors. He was the first in his market to introduce free checking accounts, certificates of deposit, automated teller machines, and credit cards. In the late 1960s Ben decided the time had come for his commercial financial institution, the Commerce Bank and Trust Company, to move out into the arena of consumer lending. But, rather than begin in the usual way by simply offering the usual range of retail loans to the general public with the hope of building a respectable volume over a period of years, Ben's entrance into the consumer lending area was noisy, spectacular, and precedent-setting.

A Giant Leap Into the World of Retail Lending

What Ben elected to do was to have his bank leap full-blown on-to the retail lending scene by purchasing outright approximately 100,000 established and active retail loan customers plus more than 10,000 collection accounts with all their inherent problems and potentials. At the outset, Ben's leap into the world of consumer lending appeared to be a master stroke that had all the earmarks of a great future success. Yet, even though things did not work out as expected, Ben's innovative venture offers a wealth of knowledge about the rights and wrongs of consumer lending and collecting.

"The College Store"

The College Store is a large retail department store opened to the public but cooperatively owned by its members—the students, faculty, alumni and alumnae, and the employees of several local universities. The College Store had fallen on hard times in the late 1960s because of a substantial delinquency problem which had been building and growing over the years of the College Store's existence as students graduated (or otherwise departed) and simultaneously walked away from the bills they owed to the College Store. This was greatly ascerbated by the "let's rip-off the establishment" attitude of the Vietnam-era students. The College Store was on the brink of filing for bankruptcy when Ben came riding to the rescue to protect the bank against the possibility of losing thousands of dollars in commercial loans given to the College Store. His rescue efforts, coincidently, gave birth to the Commerce Bank and Trust's consumer lending and collection departments. Ben reached an agreement with the College Store's board and management that he would purchase all of their outstanding loans and delinquencies (at a substantial discount, of course) in return for the exclusive right to be the single source of consumer credit for all past, present, and future College Store members—a universe of some of the wealthiest and most influential people in the United States and in the world.

Enter Master Charge®

Under Ben's guidance, the Commerce Bank and Trust became a Master Charge licensee. The College Store membership card issued annually to all members in good standing and used as a charge card in the College Store outlets (also widely accepted by local merchants for identification and to establish credit) became a combined College Store/Master Charge card with the College Store card on one side and the Master Charge card on the other. Ben chose not to become a licensee under his regional Bankcard Association which handled all of the Master Charge operations for its members, but to be an independent licensee responsible for all the charge card operations—selling the merchant accounts, issuing the cards, approving credit, creating the billing, and directing the collecting. As an independent credit card issuer, Ben had to set up the facilities to approve and administer consumer credit, the sales force to sell and service merchants, and the operations to encode, emboss, and distribute plastic cards, initiate billing, and control delinquencies. Ben was more than willing to take on all these tasks and responsibilities with their inherent problems because he saw in them the means for protecting the loans he had made to the College Store and, more importantly, the most advantageous way to become a successful retail lender.

Launching the Operation

Under the roof of the recently renovated and enlarged Commerce Bank and Trust office building, Ben assembled a coterie of consumer lenders, collectors, sales and marketing people, and support personnel that he recruited from finance companies, credit unions, and other retail credit grantors, as well as from within the Commerce Bank and Trust. These new employees numbered close to one hundred and their jobs ranged from credit reviewing to collecting, from card encoding to merchant soliciting, and from telephone credit approval to customer relations.

Initially, all active College Store members on the membership rolls (regardless of their past credit history) were mailed the combined College Store/Master Charge card with a notice stating that this was the new College Store membership card with which a member could charge purchases at the College Store as in the past, but it also had the added embellishment of permitting charge purchases at any Master Charge merchant anywhere in the world. The established member list was automatically given a credit line of $500 and informed that if they wanted a higher line they could apply for it. Here an unexpected problem developed as a number of College Store members who prided themselves as always being able to purchase for cash, angrily returned the combined cards. They insisted they wanted nothing to do with a bank charge card and wanted only their College Store membership card which they used solely to identify themselves for their College Store rebate on their cash purchases. Ben had no choice but to begin issuing College Store-only cards (which could be used only for College Store charge purchases or cash rebate identification) to those members who requested them. However, this led to a new problem. Those

College Store customers who wanted to deal only with the College Store and did not wish to be credit customers of the Commerce Bank and Trust were billed by the Commerce Bank and Trust for their annual College Store membership fee, and, if they did not pay within 25 days, they were subjected to a late charge and risked becoming a collection account. In the entire history of the College Store, no member had ever been dunned for failing to pay the annual membership fee. Instead, the College Store merely applied any past or future earned rebates to cover the fee. If they were insufficient, the membership was eventually cancelled and the remaining balance due was charged off as uncollectible.

Theft Problems

An unanticipated problem encountered with the initial mailing of the College Store/Master Charge cards was the theft of a substantial number of cards from the post office. The Commerce Bank and Trust employees in charge of card mailing quickly learned that charge cards had to be sent by costly registered mail because of a ring of credit card thieves that was operating inside the post office through which the Commerce Bank and Trust mailed its cards. Later registered mailings were staggered and routed through post offices in different locations and this eliminated any further major thefts, but at a substantially greater cost for postage and handling than had been anticipated originally. In addition, a large number of stolen cards were now in circulation and adding to the bank's collection, loss, and customer relations problems.

Collection Problems

On taking over the College Store delinquencies, bills and past due notices were created and mailed to the last known addresses of the delinquent members. In many cases, the last known address proved to be the dormitory in which a student had lived while attending college a number of years earlier. Skip-tracing became a major task of the collection department personnel. And those delinquent notices that were delivered created a storm of protest from all over America. Old grads who had not been in town for a number of years found themselves being dunned for a long-forgotten College Store membership bill that they had incurred during their senior year in college but never paid because they were leaving town and had no further intention of making College Store purchases. Bills for these delinquencies and others that went back a number of years to college undergraduate days streamed out of the Commerce Bank and Trust collection department. They were met with a counter-barrage of complaints and threats from the recipients. When the ex-College Store member failed to pay his long-forgotten membership fee of $10 within the specified 25 days, the Commerce Bank and Trust computer automatically generated a second bill with an interest charge and a strongly worded notice to pay up or else. Then, when payment still did not come in, the collection department took over. It was soon evident that a great many of the College Store's delinquent loan accounts had to be charged off by the Commerce Bank and Trust as uncollectible because a majority were for membership fees assessed by the College Store but overlooked or unwanted by the members, yet still carried on the books as past-due accounts. To sort out this portion of the College Store's delinquencies, contact the inactive members, trace current addresses, correspond with delinquents and take the time to explain the reasons for the billings, and, ultimately, charge them off as uncollectible, added unexpectedly and substantially to the Commerce Bank and Trust's costs of acquiring the College Store's membership base as retail loan customers.

Establishing Credit for New College Store Members

In addition to converting the existing College Store membership to bank credit card customers, Ben's people had to establish credit for incoming students. Applications for College Store membership (College Store/Master Charge) were automatically included in the college registration material. The incoming student then had to bring the application into any College Store outlet together with his membership fee. These were submitted to Commerce Bank and Trust loan officers who had been stationed at credit desks in the several college store's during the two weeks of student registration. Because College Store membership was automatically opened to all students regardless of their age or credit-worthiness, the loan offices could not deny credit to anyone. All students under 18 were automatically given a College Store card good for charging any purchases up to $300 at the College Store. Students between the ages of 18 and 21 were given a College Store/Master Charge card with a $300 line of credit. Those over 21 were given a $500 line or more if they requested it and were credit-worthy. Every student had to fill out a credit application and credit was approved on the spot by the loan office based solely on the information the student provided. Needless to say that few, if any, students offered adverse information which would have resulted in credit denial (except for within the College Store).

Credit Cards for Non-College Store Members

The average Commerce Bank and Trust customer, a non-College Store member, and a blue-collar worker who lived in one of the town's tenement sections, was able to apply for a Master Charge card only. He was subject to a thorough credit check and review of the information provided on his application. Because a number of the Commerce Bank and Trust loan officers were not familiar with consumer lending and the nuances in determining an applicant's credit-worthiness, Ben instituted the use of one of the first credit scoring systems. This simple and unsophisticated system enabled the loan officer to make a decision whether or not to grant credit and what the credit line should be. Use of this credit scoring system as the basis for granting or denying credit has since been shown to be ineffective. For example, it eliminated the need to make a judgment about credit-worthiness and ability to repay and gave no indication of an individual's character. Today's more sophisticated credit scoring systems can be fairly good guides to determining the credit-worthiness of a majority of applicants provided they give correct information on the application and the loan officer is able to verify the answers. (See chapter 5 for more on credit scorings.) The result of the use of a primitive credit scoring system by the Commerce Bank and Trust was that a number of unqualified applicants received Master Charge cards from the bank while a number of well-qualified applicants were denied. Within a matter of three months, the Commerce Bank and Trust Master Charge card (with or without a College Store card on the opposite face) was in use by nearly 100,000 Commerce Bank and Trust customers—the majority of whom had not previously been customers of the bank. And these cards were in use all over the free world. In one master stroke by Ben the Commerce Bank and Trust had created a world-wide network of charge customers.

Controlling the Credit Limits

To give Commerce Bank and Trust Master Charge merchants notice of the validity of the bank's cards and to keep each customer's credit within the established limits, Ben had to establish floor limits for the merchants (an amount a customer could charge without requiring the merchant to call the bank for approval). He also had to set up a 20-hour a day telephone verification service in the bank where a merchant could call to get authorization to exceed the floor limit. And, on a weekly basis, he had to print and distribute to his merchants a "stop-list" that gave the numbers of all lost or stolen cards and of those whose holders had either exceeded their credit limit or become delinquent on their payments.

This was a time of active protests against "the establishment." There were riots, marches against the Vietnam War, bank bombings and holdups by radical groups. A substantial number of these protestors had College Store/Master Charge cards which they had acquired through their College Store membership. To many of them, it became their license to strike back at "the Establishment" personified by the Commerce Bank and Trust Company. And they

The newly-established collection department became the busiest in the bank. Charges were run up at retail establishments and on airlines all over the world. Skips were commonplace as students moved from dormitories to rooming houses to communes. Monthly bills from the bank which were successfully delivered were frequently returned ripped in pieces or larded with the vilest comments, and in the bank's own free postage-paid bank-by-mail envelopes. It became common practice for foreign students to run up thousands of dollars in Master Charge purchases (by buying under the floor limits) a day or two before they permanently returned to their overseas' homes.

The Demise of the College Store/Master Charge Card

Within six months from the launching of the consumer credit operation, the Commerce Bank and Trust was reeling from uncollected loans and charge-offs. As losses mounted and no reasonable solution could be found, Ben made the painfully honest decision to take his licking and discontinue the entire credit card operation. The College Store membership lists and the attending responsibilities were returned to the College Store. All bank charge cards were cancelled and the customers notified. Only outstanding loans were maintained. Nonrecoverable losses in excess of $1,000,000 had been realized during the brief life of the experiment and, if the operation had continued, projected losses of $4,000,000 for the next twelve months were anticipated. Unquestionably, Ben had a good idea and had saved the College Store from bankruptcy and protected the loans that the Commerce Bank and Trust had made to the College Store, but the move into a consumer credit operation by way of a credit card proved to be one that was launched at the wrong time and under the wrong circumstances. Still, there were many positive results. Commerce Bank and Trust had established a battle-wise and experienced retail lending and collection facility. The bank was able to retain a fair number of the original 100,000 card holders as both savers and retail loan customers. On the heels of the College Store/Master Charge debacle, Ben quickly turned the attention of his now-established consumer lenders to the generation of all types of profitable consumer loans. The bank soon became a recognized consumer lender in its market area with a substantial share of the market.

An Idea That Paid Off

Another of Ben's ideas did pay off handsomely for the Commerce Bank and Trust Company during the same period as the College Store/Master Charge failure. Like most commercial banks, it was heavily involved with auto loans on a floor-planning basis (financing the auto dealer's bulk stock purchases). To move into retail auto loans in a big way (Ben thought "big" in everything), Ben approached the largest automobile club in the United States. He proposed that they offer their members low-cost auto loans as a membership benefit. The club would promote the loans under its own name and send all applications it received to the Commerce Bank and Trust Company. The bank would, in turn, issue the loan to a credit-worthy club member at a below-market rate. The club would receive a small commission or finder's fee for every loan written to a member. The automobile club bought Ben's idea and promoted the new member discount auto loan to their hundreds of thousands of members. In a brief time, the Commerce Bank and Trust built a very profitable, high quality portfolio of retail auto loans.

Your Own Resident Banking Innovator

While not too many potential or actual consumer lenders are blessed with the services of a resident banking innovator like Ben, even ordinary folk who have the desire to move their businesses into the highly profitable consumer lending arena—or who are looking for ways to improve their present retail lending and collection operations—can do so. With a little bit of common sense, good advanced planning, and the application of the practices and procedures presented in this book, retail lending can become a safe and profitable income source for most institutions. Ben's adventures with the College Store/Master Charge operation offer a unique insight into the actual establishment of a start-up consumer lending and collection facility together with its pitfalls and attainments. From it and the information that follows, the tyro or the veteran consumer lender or collector will find many of the answers to help him or her develop a successful retail lending and collecting operation.

2

A Review of Consumer Loans

Ben was a proponent of the basic idea that the only products financial institutions have to sell are *dollars* and *services and there is no difference between one institution's bills and coins and another's!* The only disparity between a small loan company, a brokerage house, an insurance company, a gambling casino, a money market fund, a bank, or a credit card issuer, is the manner in which they package the money they sell: their *services*. Their ultimate product is the money they offer to the public either as interest paid on dollars invested or as dollars packaged into loans of various types which produce earnings for the lender. Future growth for any business entity that deals in dollars will come only by creating and offering more attractive and profitable services tied to those dollars.

So, the creditor who wishes to grow should give constant thought to improving existing services or creating unique and varied

11

services. The goal of every credit granter should be to improve the volume and profitability of its business and increase the number of productive customers, especially in the retail credit area. That's what Ben did when he arranged to take over the College Store's accounts. However, most lenders don't have a Ben to do this, so they must look to their consumer credit department managers and their staffs for such guidance. Any improvements or differences in the credit services offered are the responsibility of the individuals who sell them.

THREE BASIC TYPES OF CONSUMER CREDIT

Throughout this book, we will be discussing both retail credit and retail lending. However, it should be recognized that we are referring to personal credit in general and that the subjects discussed apply to all types of personal credit and that the words "loan" and "credit" are interchangeable for the most part.

There are three types of personal credit: credit for services, retail credit, and personal loans. Creditors (lenders) usually extend only one of these three basic types of consumer credit.

1. *Service credit* is extended by doctors, hospitals, dentists, lawyers, architects, landlords, and other professional individuals or organizations who extend credit for their services and then bill after the fact for the services rendered.
2. *Retail credit* is extended to consumers for the purchase of merchandise. It takes one of three forms: installment plan, regular charge, and revolving charge. Under the installment plan an item is purchased on credit, a down payment is usually paid, and a note is signed to secure the loan. Payback is then made monthly for a predetermined period of time. With a regular charge the merchandise purchased on credit is billed for and repaid in 30 days. With the revolving charge, there is usually no down payment and if the charge is not paid in full in 30 days it is converted into a long-term loan paid back in installments.
3. A *personal loan* is when cash rather than merchandise or service is advanced.

TYPES OF CONSUMER LOANS

There are a number of different consumer loans that can be considered by an institution. The individual in charge of lending operations should examine the type of loans now being offered as well as those that are not. Some lenders lose out on the possibility of greater profits for their institutions by restricting themselves to one or more types of consumer loans. For example, many savings and loan associations offer only savings-secured loans and home mortgages. Some retailers restrict credit only to charge plate purchasers. But almost all consumer loans can be profitable to the lender if they are understood thoroughly, packaged properly, priced wisely, and managed correctly. This book concerns itself solely with retail or consumer loans. Except for passing reference, it does not deal with business or commercial credit or with residential or commercial mortgages. These pages will cover those loans (both secured and unsecured) that are offered to the general public by banks, credit unions, finance companies, insurance firms, credit card issuers, and retail organizations that sell their products or services on credit. For the most part, these are loans of a short-term nature (usually for a period of several months to five years), with fixed interest (although the introduction of variable interest rates for short-term consumer loans is being considered by many lenders and is actually in use by a few progressive lenders). Short-term loans call for regularly scheduled payments of both principal and interest as opposed to other types of loans which call either for a lump sum payment of both principal and interest at a future date or the payment of all interest up front at the time the loan is granted with the principal to be paid later as agreed. Basically, credit can be put into two categories: open-end and closed-end.

Open-End Credit

Open-end credit loans are those that are characterized by a predetermined maximum amount which the borrower can have from the lender (a line of credit) and can call upon as needed or wanted in increments and then repay in regular installments. Examples are credit cards, department store charge plates, and check overdraft accounts that allow a borrower to write checks for more then the actual amount on deposit in the checking account. Open-end credit can be used repeatedly without the necessity of applying for a new loan each time the borrower needs additional funds until the prearranged borrowing limit is reached.

Closed-End Credit

Closed-end credit loans are those that are granted for only a specific time period. The number of payments to be made, the total amount of such payments, and the payment due dates are all agreed upon between the lender and the borrower in advance of the loan being made. Closed-end credit is usually granted to borrowers who need a large amount of money for some major purchase or expense such as the purchase of an automobile or the financing of a vacation trip. Also, any loan that is to be repaid in one lump sum at a predetermined future date is considered closed-end credit.

Personal Installment Loans (Unsecured)
This is the most common type of consumer loan and can be either open-end or closed-end. In either form, it can be offered by virtually all lenders, not only financial institutions but also retailers who extend credit to their customers and permit them to repay either on an open-end or closed-end loan basis. As the name implies, an unsecured personal installment loan is granted to the borrower on the basis of his or her personal character and reputation plus the perceived capacity to repay in the future. There is no collateral assigned to the lender to secure such a loan.

The Unsecured Closed-End Loan
A personal, unsecured, closed-end installment loan is usually granted for a short period of time ranging from six months to five years with the average being two and one-half years. Repayment is made in equal amounts unless the loan is a variable rate loan in which case loan payments may go up or down on occasion. A typical personal unsecured installment loan usually carries a higher interest rate than one that is secured by collateral and so carries little or no risk for the lender. Typically, such a loan might be written for a principal sum of $1,000, for a period of 24 months, at a discount rate of 8½% (the equivalent simple annual percentage rate would be 18.73%). This loan would be repaid in 24 monthly payments of

$97.72 which will return to the lender the original $1,000 principal plus $272.27 in accrued interest.

The Unsecured Open-End Loan

A personal, unsecured, open-end loan may be granted for a specified time (for example, the expiration date on a credit card) or with no set time limit for use. Nothing is paid on the loan and no interest is charged until the loan is actually activated. Thus, an individual who has overdraft loan privileges on his or her checking account might not make use of it for two or three years after it had been approved. Until the time of the actual use of the credit, there is no charge for the credit line. However, the lender must have disclosed at the time the credit line was established the method that would be used to calculate the finance charge and when the finance charge would actually begin. The open-end loan is different from the closed-end loan in that the outstanding principal can change from month to month and the amount repaid can vary depending on the principal balance, the system the lender uses to calculate the balance on which the finance charge will be assessed, and the inclination of the borrower to repay the minimum payment due or a greater amount which would then reduce the principal on which the finance charge is based. For example, one creditor might add finance charges after subtracting any payments made during the billing period. This is called the "adjusted balance method." Another lender might give no credit for payments made during the billing period; this is the "previous balance method." A third lender might use the "average daily balance method" whereby the balance owed for each day in the billing period is added and then divided by the number of days in the billing period to create an average charge for the funds borrowed during the billing period.

OPEN-END CREDIT BILLING SYSTEM EXAMPLES.

	Adjusted Balance	Previous Balance	Average Daily Balance
Monthly Interest Rate	1½%	1½%	1½%
Previous Balance	$500	$500	$500
Payments	$400	$400	$400
Interest Charge	$1.50 ($100x1.5%)	$7.50 ($500x1.5%)	$4.50 (average balance of $300x1.5%)

As noted, the lender must also disclose to the borrower at the time the open-end credit line is established when finance charges begin. Usually, in the case of checking account overdraft credit, finance charges begin on the day the loan is initiated, whereas in the case of many credit cards, the finance charge goes into effect 30 days after a loan is initiated thus giving the borrower a grace period where he or she has free use of the lender's funds.

Reasons for Granting Unsecured Credit

Personal unsecured loans are generally granted for any legitimate legal or moral purpose the borrower has in mind and, in the case of closed-end loans, has disclosed to the lender. The most common reasons for an unsecured personal installment loan are to repay a number of accumulated small bills, to repay unexpected medical or repair bills, to purchase clothing, furniture, or appliances, or to finance education, a vacation trip or some other activity. Usually unacceptable reasons for granting an unsecured loan would be for gambling, investing, or providing a down-payment for a car or a mortgage. Guidelines for granting an unsecured loan are those established by the lender and in accordance with local, state, and federal regulations that govern public lending policies and practices. Such regulations usually specify the criteria the lender can apply to determine the borrower's credit worthiness, ability, and capacity to repay the loan, the limits on the amount of money that can be borrowed, the terms of the loan, and the interest that can be charged, plus late fees, charge penalties, collection and legal costs, and other methods that can be used to collect the loan if it becomes delinquent.

Secured (Collateral) Demand Loans

The most common secured consumer loans are those given against funds on deposit in a financial institution. The next common type are those loans that are given for the purchase of motor vehicles, mobile homes, recreation vehicles, or boats with the vehicles as the collateral. A lender may be willing to accept other collateral as security such as stocks, bonds, or precious metals. The security of these tangibles (with the occasional exception of motor vehicles which depreciate with time and use) is usually more than adequate to return to the lender the entire cost of the loan (including the interest) if there is a default. Such a loan is written so that the ownership of the collateral can be transferred to the lender if the loan is not repaid according to the agreed terms and conditions under which it was written. A collateral loan is usually payable on demand but with a fixed interest repayment schedule. If the schedule is not met, it results in demand for payment in full by the lender, and if not forthcoming, the collateral is converted into cash and applied to pay off the loan in its entirety. Sometimes, too, the principal may be repayable on a regular basis with the interest payable only in arrears.

Because the loan is secured, therefore theoretically risk free, the criteria the lender uses to determine the debtor's ability to repay may not be quite as strict for an unsecured loan. And, the interest rate charged by the lender may not be quite as high as that for an unsecured loan. Additionally, the lender seldom cares about the purpose of the loan since, in effect, the borrower is using his or her own funds.

Education Loans

Under federal and state laws, a financial institution may offer a special type of loan to be used by the borrower to pay tuition charges and other expenses at an approved higher educational institution. Such a loan is made available to qualified students or their parents under the United States government's Higher Education Loan Program (HELP) or under a similar state sponsored program. And, as an added incentive to lenders, the government pays the lender for the use of the funds.

The usual criteria for an education loan requires that the applicant:

1. Have a certification that he or she is enrolled or has been accepted for enrollment as at least a half-time student in an approved educational institution and is in satisfactory academic standing with the institution.
2. Is a permanent resident of the United States or intends to become one or of the state that is sponsoring the program or is attending an institution in the sponsoring state.
3. Is qualified for eligibility for the loan under the criteria established by either the federal or state regulations.

The typical HELP loan is an unsecured personal loan. It must be written according to specific guidelines (including rates of interest and terms) set by the sponsoring agency and must use their application forms and notes. Funds have to be dispensed as directed by the sponsor. The lender is responsible for collecting the payments and administering the loan which is usually guaranteed 100% by either the federal or the state government agency.

While the student is in school, no amortization of the principal is called for and, in most instances, the government pays the interest to the lender quarterly. When the student leaves school, he or she repays both the principal and the interest through monthly payments to the lender.

Advantages to Lenders

Because the education loan is guaranteed in the event of default by the student, the lending institution has a risk-free investment opportunity. In addition, there are now programs that make it possible for lenders to "sell" their education loans to other institutions and thus, quickly recover their principal plus interest for reinvesting. Also, the return on education loans in recent years has been far greater than the actual interest charged to the borrower because of subsidiary payments made to match prevailing interest rates also made to the lender by the sponsoring government agency. A number of financial institutions have concentrated on offering education loans in recent years and have realized substantial returns from them because they are similar to a variable-rate consumer loan where the interest rate keeps pace with the national interest rate barometers.

Variable-Rate Installment Loans

New on the scene are variable-rate, short-term consumer loans. Until the mid-1970s, interest rates were fairly stable in the United States and a lender could be quite confident that if he granted a loan at 5% discount interest for three years, an 11.5% return three years later would still be a profitable investment. That is no longer true. Lenders have seen interest rates go into double digits while they have continued to have their money loaned out for single digit returns. Rates now can swing dramatically on a weekly basis whereas in previous years changes were only in very small increments and over a long period of time. Because of this drastically altered economy, in those states where it is legal to do so prudent lenders are instituting variable rate consumer loans.

The variable rate loan can be a viable instrument for any lender not restricted by a usury law which limits loan interest to an unrealistic predetermined percentage and where the state laws permit either payment amounts to change or the life of the loan to extend or contract beyond the terms and conditions set in the original contract (See figures 2–1 and 2–2).

How the Variable Rate Loan Works

The loan contract signed by the borrower contains a clause that gives the lender the right to increase or decrease the interest payments on a predetermined time schedule based on an increase or decline in some established rate index (such as the "Prime Rate" or a U.S. Treasury bill rate). There is usually a "floor" and a "ceiling" indicated by which amount the rate can rise or fall each time an adjustment is made, and a notice (usually 30 days) is given to the borrower before the adjustment takes place. To make it easier on the borrower, the upward or downward adjustment is not always made by increasing or decreasing the payment amounts. Rather, the length of the loan can be adjusted to accommodate the repayment that must be made. In all cases, when the rate is changed, a new disclosure must be sent to the borrower so he or she knows exactly what his or her annual percentage rate is and what other new terms and conditions now apply. Normally, too, when the borrower is informed of a change in rate, he or she can also elect to pay the loan off in full at the original rate without penalty.

Home Improvement Loans

This book does not concern itself with residential mortgage lending but it does cover home improvement loans. These are loans granted to home owners for the purpose of either repairing or remodeling their residences or other real property they may own. A home improvement loan is usually secured by the real estate for the difference between the present balance of any existing mortgage(s) and the original mortgage amount(s). The amount that is lent for a

FIGURE 2-1

Date: _____

VARIABLE RATE NOTE

DEFINITIONS. This Note is a binding contract. Your signature makes You responsible to repay according to the terms described below. The words "You", "Your" or "Yours" means each and all persons (jointly and severally) who sign as borrower, co-borrower, guarantor or surety. The words "Bank" or "We" means _____ or its assigns. Your Disclosure Statement should be referred to for additional information. It is incorporated herein by reference.

PROMISE AND TERMS OF REPAYMENT. For value received, You promise to pay the Bank, or order, the Principal Sum of $_____, plus interest, from the date of this Note at _____ % per year or at the adjusted rate in accordance with the terms of this Note. You will repay the loan in _____ consecutive monthly installments of $_____, or as adjusted, due on the same day of each month beginning _____ 19 _____. Monthly payments will be applied first to interest accrued at the time Your payment is received, and then to the remaining unpaid principal. You will pay any balance due under the Note in full on the last payment date or when the loan is paid off, whichever occurs first.

EARLY AND LATE PAYMENTS. Your Finance Charge and Total of Payments are computed using the simple interest method. Interest accrues on a daily basis on the outstanding principal balance. Any monthly payment You make earlier than the specified payment date will decrease the Finance Charge and the Total of Payments. Any payment made later than the specified payment date will increase the Finance Charge and Total of Payments. If the latter event occurs, You agree to pay any additional amounts along with the final installment payment.

PREPAYMENT. You may prepay the unpaid principal balance in part or in full at any time, without penalty. Upon prepayment in full, any unearned portion of Life and/or Accident & Health Insurance Premiums will be refunded according to the SUM OF THE DIGITS METHOD, commonly known as the RULE OF 78's.

VARIABLE RATE NOTE. This means the rate of interest You pay may increase or decrease over the term of the loan in relation to changes in the Index Rate. Any decrease in the interest rate required by the terms of this Note shall be mandatory. The "Index Rate" shall mean the interest rate is charging on loans similar to the type represented by this Note. If the Bank is not offering similar type loans on the day the Review Date occurs, then the "Alternate Index Rate" used shall be a rate two percentage points (2%) above the Federal National Mortgage Association's (FNMA) rate for first mortgage participation loans requiring thirty (30) day mandatory delivery. If FNMA discontinues the publication of the "Alternate Index Rate", the Bank shall notify You of the new Index Rate it has chosen. One (1) year from the date of this Note, and at the end of each 12 month period thereafter, You will have an Adjustment Date. Any change in the interest rate will take effect on the Adjustment Date. Forty-five (45) days prior to the Adjustment Date will be Your Review Date. Any adjustment made to Your existing rate will reflect the Index Rate in effect on the first day of the month in which the Review Date occurs. No adjustment in the rate of interest will be made if the adjustment would be less than one quarter of one percentage point (1/4%). No single adjustment will change your interest rate by more than two percentage points (2%) from your existing rate at the time of the Adjustment Date. No adjustment will be made which increases the interest rate higher than the Bank is allowed to charge under applicable law at the time of the adjustment. Any adjustment in the interest rate charged will result in a change in the monthly payment to insure the complete amortization of the loan according to its original term.

NOTICE OF ADJUSTMENT. You will be notified by mail that Your rate is being adjusted. An adjustment will become effective on the Adjustment Date specified in the notice. The adjustment will not take effect less than thirty (30) days before the notice is mailed to You. It will be mailed to the address below. It is your responsibility to notify the Bank in writing if Your mailing address changes during the term of this loan.

Loan No.

Check if applicable
☐ If checked here the Bank now holds a mortgage on the property described in the HOME IMPROVEMENT LOAN section above. You agree that this Note will be secured by that mortgage but, in accordance with Massachusetts General Laws, Chapter 183 Section 28A, only to the extent that the loan amount outstanding on this Note, when added to amounts due under that mortgage, do not exceed the amount originally secured by that mortgage.

BANK'S SECURITY INTEREST-SECOND MORTGAGE
Check if Applicable
☐ (A)   You agree that Your obligations under this Note will be secured by Mortgage on real estate located at _____
_____ more fully described in the Mortgage. This Mortgage will also secure any additional amounts the Bank loans to You, at any time after the recording of the Mortgage, to pay for repairs, improvements, or replacements, or for taxes or other municipal, liens, charges or assessments. These additional loans will not secure a Mortgage in an amount greater than the original Amount Financed under this Note.

(B)   You also agree to provide property insurance on the Mortgaged Property and provide the Bank with an insurance policy in the amount of coverage required by the Bank, including flood insurance if required. The Bank shall be named as an insured secured party. The Bank does not sell such insurance. You may obtain it from anyone who is acceptable to the Bank.

If you sell or transfer the property described in the HOME IMPROVEMENT LOAN OR BANK'S SECURITY INTEREST sections, You agree to pay off any remaining unpaid balance along with any accrued interest at that time.

DEFAULT. You will be in **default** if:
(A)   Any monthly installment (or monthly adjusted installment) is not paid on time and remains unpaid for more than thirty (30) days.
(B)   You fail to comply with the provisions of this Note.
(C)   You fail to comply with the provisions of any mortgage securing this Note.
(D)   You file bankruptcy or bankruptcy proceedings are instituted against You.
(E)   Anyone else attempts by legal proceedings to acquire the property.
(F)   You have given any false information on Your loan application.

If You are in default You agree to:
(A)   Immediately pay the Bank the unpaid balance of the Note with accrued interest.
(B)   Pay the Bank its costs of collecting amounts due including reasonable fees and expenses charged by the Bank's attorney.

If You are in default the Bank may:
(A)   Declare the balance of Note due immediately.
(B)   Sell any property secured by this Note.

SET-OFF. If You are in default, You agree that the Bank may set-off and apply any and all deposits or other sums in the Bank's possession or to be credited to You, to repay the Note without first resorting to, and regardless of the adequacy of, any other security.

WAIVER. Each party signing as maker, guarantor, endorser, surety or otherwise waives demand, presentment, protest, notice of any kind and all suretyship defenses. Each party also assents to any extension, modification or amendment of the Note and to any substitution, exchange, or release of capital held by the Bank. The Bank may accept late or deferred payments, partial payments, check or money orders marked "payment in full" without waiving any of the Bank's rights under the Note.

APPLICABLE LAW. This Note shall be governed by _____ law. If any provision of this Note conflicts with any applicable law or regulation, that provision shall be deemed modified to be consistent with the law or regulation. The provision will be deleted if such modification is impossible. All Your other obligations under the Note, as modified, shall remain the same.

READ CAREFULLY

You should read this Note and other related documents carefully. Your signature makes You legally responsible to fulfill all the provisions of this Note. Your signature means You have received a completed copy. This Note shall have the effect of a sealed instrument.

_____   _____
Borrower (Signature)   Address

_____   _____
Borrower (Signature)   Address

FIGURE 2–2

VARIABLE RATE – SIMPLE INTEREST

ANNUAL PERCENTAGE RATE The cost of your credit as a yearly rate.	FINANCE CHARGE The dollar amount the credit will cost you.	Amount Financed The amount of credit provided to you or on your behalf.	Total of Payments The amount you will have paid after you have made all payments as scheduled.
%	$	$	$

Your payment schedule will be:

Number of Payments	Amount of Payments	When Payments are Due
	$	
	$	
	$	
	$	
	$	

INSURANCE: Credit life insurance and credit disability insurance are not required to obtain credit, and will not be provided unless you sign and agree to pay the additional cost.

Type	Premium	Term	Signature
Credit Life	$		I want to apply for credit life insurance. Signature
Credit Disability	$		I want to apply for credit disability insurance. Signature

VARIABLE RATE: The annual percentage rate may increase during the term of this transaction if the Index Rate increases. The initial Index Rate is the rate the Bank is charging on similar type loans when your Review Date occurs 45 days prior to the actual Adjustment Date. The rate may not be adjusted more than once a year and may not increase more than two percentage points (2%) annually. Any increase will take the form of higher payments. If the interest rate increases by one percentage point (1%) in one year, your regular payment would increase to $ _____ .

PREPAYMENT: If you pay off early, you will not have to pay a penalty.
If you pay off early, you will not be entitled to a refund of part of the finance charge.

ASSUMPTION: Someone buying your house cannot assume the remainder of the mortgage on the original terms.

INSURANCE: You may obtain property insurance from anyone you want who is acceptable to the Bank.

SECURITY: You are giving a security interest in real estate located at _____

and also in accounts and other property held by the Bank.

Collateral securing other loans with us may also secure this loan.

FILING FEES: $ _____

RECORDING FEES: $ _____

See your contract documents for any additional information about nonpayment, default, any required repayment in full before the scheduled date, and prepayment refunds and penalties.

(e means an estimate)

Itemization of Amount Financed of $

$ _____ Amount given to you directly

$ _____ Amount paid on your account

Amounts Paid to Others on Your Behalf

$ _____ to _____

$ _____ to _____

Prepaid Finance Charge: $ _____

$ _____ to _____

OTHER DISCLOSURES: _____

I/We acknowledge receipt today of (a) completed copy (ies) of this statement.

Date: _____   Signature (s): _____

home improvement loan is normally greater than that which can be borrowed through an unsecured personal loan and it is granted for a longer period of time and at a different interest rate. Such a loan is often based on an estimate of the cost of the work to be done and the materials to be used. The estimate is provided by a reputable builder, contractor, and/or retailer of home building supplies. For security, the lenders normally record their liens on the deed for the property. (See figure 2–3, Agreement Not to Encumber.) Or, even though there can be an inferred lien by law without a second mortgage the lender may use a security agreement, a second mortgage, a trust deed, or a financing statement to further protect the loan.

A lender may also grant a home improvement loan under FHA Title I. This loan creates an inferred lien on the property being improved if no prior lien exists on the real estate and if the amount advanced to the borrower does not exceed the difference between the original amount and the present mortgage balance. The United States government guarantees 90% of the balance due on FHA Title I Home Improvement Loans.

Secured Loans vs. Unsecured Loans

When home mortgages are excluded from consideration, the majority of loans granted in the United States by all lenders (banks, retailers, finance companies) are unsecured. This has come about because of the introduction of credit cards. Today, most Americans purchase gasoline, air travel, mail order items, medical services, retail merchandise, and restaurant meals on credit by creating unsecured loans through the use of plastic cards. The dollar volume of these loans combined with the cash loans offered by banks and finance companies greatly exceeds the dollar value of those loans secured by real or personal property or by goods or chattel. For this reason, the lender should be extremely cautious in granting credit by insisting on thorough documentation and detailed examination of every loan applicant's credit history and ability to repay. The same caution holds true for secured loans because it is possible in certain

FIGURE 2-3

AGREEMENT NOT TO ENCUMBER OR TRANSFER PROPERTY

KNOW ALL MEN BY THESE PRESENTS: That the undersigned, hereinafter called the "Borrowers", for and in consideration of the some of   dollars and other good and valuable considerations unto them in hand paid, the receipt whereof is hereby acknowledged and for the purpose of inducing the
a Corporation duly organized under the laws of the Commonwealth of Massachusetts and having its usual place of business at   Massachusetts, hereinafter called the "Bank", to grant credit to the undersigned, under a promissory note in the sum of   dated   , the undersigned hereby jointly and severally covenant, promise and agree as follows, to wit:

1. So long as the note hereinabove referred to, or any portion thereof, or any extension or renewal thereof, and also any and all other indebtedness of the Borrowers, or either of them, to said Bank, whether joint or several, heretofore or hereafter incurred, of any nature whatsoever, shall remain unpaid, either before or after maturity thereof, the said Borrowers will do the following things, to wit:

   (a) Pay promptly, when due, all fire and windstorm insurance premiums, taxes, assessments, dues and charges of every kind imposed or levied upon their real and personal property, prior to the time when any such sums shall become delinquent or in default; and

   (b) Promptly pay, when due, any and all sums due and owing on any mortgage, or other encumbrance, on the property hereinafter described and will never suffer or permit any mortgage lien, or encumbrance, thereon to become delinquent or go into default.

2. The Borrowers agree that they will not, without first procuring the consent in writing of the said Bank, hereafter create or permit any lien or other encumbrance to exist on their property, real or personal, now owned or hereafter acquired by them, including, but not limited to, the property hereafter described.

3. The Borrowers agree that they shall not have the privilege, nor will they sell, transfer, assign, hypothecate, or in any manner whatever dispose of the property or any interest therein, owned by them, including specifically, but not limited to, the following real estate situate, to wit: address of Real Estate

Recorded   Book   Page

so long as any indebtedness or obligation shall remain unpaid as hereinabove referred to in Paragraph 1.

4. If the Borrowers shall default in any of the covenants, promises and agreements herein contained to be made, done, and performed by the, or if they shall attempt to transfer, sell, hypothecate, dispose of or encumber any of the property of the Borrowers without first procuring the consent in writing of the Bank therefor, then, in either or any of such events, the Bank may, in addition to any and all other rights, which the Bank may have, declare the entire remaining upaid principal and interest of any such obligations or indebtedness, then remaining unpaid to the Bank, due and payable forthwith and shall, as security for the payment thereof, have a lien on all of the property of the Borrowers, both real and personal, including but not limited to the real estate hereinabove described, which lien may be enforced by foreclosure in the same manner as a mortgage may be enforced for default, and the Borrowers further agree that, within ten (10) days of a demand made upon them, they will execute and deliver a formal Statutory Form Mortgage Deed to   of the property herein described, which will recite the terms of the note given to secure the loan granted to the Borrowers by

The undersigned hereby acknowledges receipt of a true, correct and complete copy of this agreement.

IN WITNESS WHEREOF, the undersigned have hereunto set their hands and seals at County of   , Commonwealth of Massachusetts this   day of
, 19

Signed, sealed and delivered in the
presence of:

                                                   Borrowers

State of Massachusetts, County of   ss.

On this   day of   19   , before me personally appeared
to me known to be the persons described in and who executed the foregoing instrument, and acknowledged that they executed the same as their free act and deed.

                                         Notary Public

My commission expires

cases for collateral to disappear or to substantially decline in value thus making it inadequate to cover the loan in the event of a default.

The importance to every lender—whether granting secured or unsecured consumer loans—of having a reliable system for evaluating credit applicants is set forth in the following chapters.

3

Creating The Retail Credit Department

THE NEED FOR A SYSTEM

As Ben knew so well when he set about creating his bank's retail credit operation, there is a carefully-calculated system behind every successful consumer lending or credit department: a system for establishing and maintaining good relationships with borrowers; for taking and processing applications; for issuing money and extending credit; for billing and transacting payments; for collecting past due accounts; for keeping track of all information connected with each customer's account. Even the single-proprietor business will benefit from a well-defined credit system. Such a system may be either manual or computerized. Whichever way a lender chooses, the basics are still the same, only the manner in which the information is maintained is different. (See figure 3–1.) In this chapter, the

FIGURE 3–1.   The retail credit cycle.

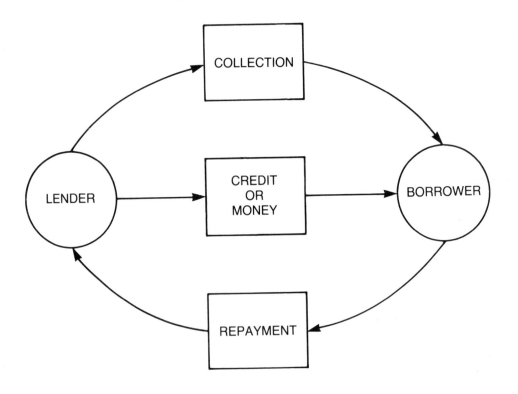

reader (if operating a computer-based system) should substitute "computer," "word processor," or "data bank" for "file" or "record" or "index card." The vast majority of retailers and financial institutions already offer some form of consumer credit or lending. So, whether the lender is establishing a totally new credit operation or just looking for ways to improve the existing one, the primary task is to create a total system to properly handle each and every consumer credit account you create. By setting policies and following set procedures for granting credit, the wise businessperson helps to insure his or her success and profitability. A robust department requires three elements: people, policies, procedures, and each of these should be worked out in detail when putting together or revamping a consumer credit department. (See figure 3–2.)

FIGURE 3–2.   *Retail Credit System*—A 3-legged stool requiring people, policies, and procedures to support it.

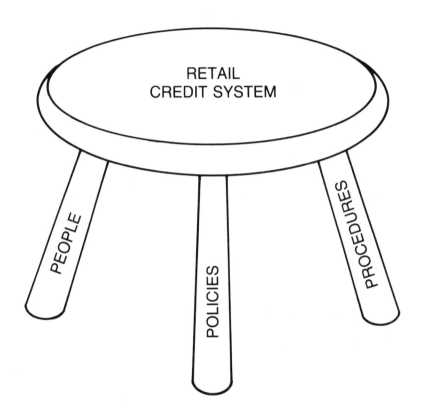

It Starts With the Right People

In a retail credit operation the right people on the job can insure the profitability (which is the measure of success) of the operation. The wrong people on the job can cut off profitable loan business either by turning the right borrowers off or down. Whether the business extending the credit is a one-person operation or a multi-employee one, it is the responsibility of the person in charge of the company or institution to insure the profitability of the consumer credit department by assigning the best qualified individual to run it. A good consumer credit or loan manager must have a multitude of talents that range from the ability to empathize with others to the intuition to identify a good credit risk from a poor one. In the case of the one-person business, that person must look to himself or herself to determine if he or she has the right attributes to take loan applications with equanimity and aptness, to practically evaluate the borrower's credit worthiness, to reliably maintain the credit records, and to energetically manage the billing and the collection when necessary—in addition to all the other demands of running the day-to-day business operations. In such a case, it might be better for the individual owner to rely on an outside credit granter to provide the retail credit service. The multi-employee organization must look for the needed qualities in the one employee it puts in charge of its lending operations or in the several employees to which it assigns each of the several lending functions.

Training the Lending Personnel

People are the heart of every operation—except those run entirely by computers and, even then, it takes people to properly plan and program the computers. So, unless a business is organized so that a credit application is taken by an automated teller, then processed through a computer which makes the decision to "lend or not to lend," the personnel who will make up the consumer credit department should be trained to run the operation properly.

Personnel training is simply teaching the concepts and skills needed so employees are able to perform their jobs satisfactorily. These accomplishments include knowledge of how the department functions, how to perform each clerical task required, how to operate any business machine which might be used in performing the job, and how to serve customers with friendliness, fairness, and tact.

Just as Ben had to educate a number of employees quickly in new consumer credit methods, techniques, and laws, so it may be necessary for some new entries into the retail lending marketplace to train their personnel. This book is not an employee training manual so we do not offer or suggest training methods for employers to use. Rather, we suggest that the employer determine what training methods to use, while this book suggests the many things an employee of a credit or loan department should know.

Training of credit or loan department personnel is needed so the employer can educate them about state and federal laws governing consumer credit and the policies and procedures followed by the creditor. Proper training will minimize customer problems, reduce future delinquencies, and insure efficient operations. In addition, good advanced training of personnel, will teach them how to take advantage of cross-sell opportunities so other services offered by the creditor can be sold successfully to credit applicants.

The Objectives of an Employee Training Program

Before launching a consumer credit training program, employers should set forth the objectives they wish to achieve. Knowing the objectives will help determine the training methods to be used. Each lender will undoubtedly have objectives that he or she wishes her or his department and employees to master, but the following are offered as typical of most retail lending operations.

1. To sell employees on the merits of consumer lending and the importance of the service they are performing.
2. To educate employees on the laws, policies, and procedures governing consumer credit services.
3. To teach employees to sell their services to others (families, friends, acquaintances).
4. To instruct employees on how to capitalize on cross-sell opportunities.
5. To inform employees about customer problems inherent in consumer lending.
6. To reinforce existing employee knowledge.
7. To emphasize the need for more personalized customer service and how to provide it.
8. To stress the need for employees to keep current records and to maintain extremely accurate records.

The Lending Policies

Lending policies are those rules an employer will lay down which will guide and be followed by all lenders in his or her employ.

In turn, they will be applied to all credit applicants without exception. These policies should be in writing, properly endorsed and approved by the employer's policy-making body, and be in such a form that they can be made available to any borrower on request in compliance with state and federal laws governing equal lending opportunity and truth-in-lending requirements. Corporate lending policies should cover:

1. Who is eligible for credit
2. The critieria to be applied to determine credit eligibility
3. The practices that must be followed by the applicant when applying for credit
4. The available types of consumer loans
5. The dollar limits (minimums and maximums)
6. The methods by which interest will be levied
7. Any finance and/or service charges
8. How payments are expected to be made
9. Collection procedures to be followed in the event of a default
10. Corporate, federal, state, or other authorities to whom a borrower can appeal in the event of a dispute or question.

Who is Eligible for Credit?

Generally speaking, there can be no discrimination when offering credit to the public. As a rule you should accept a loan application from any individual *regardless of age (except minors), circumstance, or eligibility* who desires to apply to your institution for credit. If you deny anyone this basic right to apply, you run the risk of legal action by either or both state and federal authorities charged with enforcing various consumer protection laws now in force in the United States. But once the application has been received by you, you can accept or reject it depending on whether or not the applicant meets the criteria you have established for credit eligibility. For example, you can restrict loans to those who are members of your society or association, you can restrict loans based on age (minors), residence, mental capacity, income, or credit history. As long as your lending policies are in writing and are applied without exception regardless of race, sex, religion, or age if not a minor, you can restrict the extension of credit by your institution only to those individuals whom you desire to serve. Your institution might elect as a policy to extend credit only to those individuals who have lived in a clearly-defined market area for a predetermined minimum time period, or only to those persons whose annual income from all sources is at least $15,000, or only to those who are members in good standing of the Grand Army of the Republic. The simple key to avoiding legal problems in connection with establishing credit is to accept loan applications from anyone who wishes to apply regardless of eligibility. Then the lender should judge the eligibility of the applicant against the criteria that has been previously established by his or her institution and which should be even-handedly followed by all who have lending authority. To deviate from the established policies and to make exceptions for any reason is to create cause for legal and punitive action by federal and/or state authorities.

The Criteria to Determine Credit Eligibility

Criteria will differ from institution to institution and from lender to lender. The state and federal authorities have for the most part left it up to each lender to determine the specific criteria he or she can apply and expect a borrower to meet with the exceptions of race, creed, color, sex, or age (if not a minor). Thus, lenders can set up their own criteria for income, residence, credit history, financial obligations, and occupation. The only rule lenders must follow is that once they have established their criteria, they must apply it equally to all until such time as they may alter the criteria.

The Dollar Limit
As part of its lending policy, an institution should determine the minimum and maximum dollar amounts (or the extent of credit) that will be permitted for any borrower and the circumstances by which limits can be extended. For example, the institution might determine that its maximum unsecured personal loan will be $5000 to any individual who meets its basic standards. However, if the individual earns at least twice the minimum annual income requirement and has outstanding debts equal to no more than 25% of his or her total annual net income, he or she is eligible to borrow up to $10,000.

On the other hand, a lender should determine its cost of lending and, as a result, establish the minimum amount it can afford to lend—either to break even or to make a minimum profit. Obviously, if it costs an institution $35 just to put a loan on its books and to administer it, it should not lend an amount as small as $100 which will return far less than $35 in interest and finance charge income to the lender. In such a case, a lender might establish a minimum loan limit at $500 for one year or less.

Applying Interest to the Loan

The interest the lender wishes to charge the borrower for the use of funds or for purchasing on credit can take many forms and can be computed in a number of ways. The lender should give careful consideration to the several options available and make a determination about the interest that will be applied and what type of interest it will be. Whatever form it may take, the lender is obligated under the Truth-In-Lending law to provide the borrower with a complete explanation of the interest charged and the Annual Percentage Rate (APR) that must be paid.

Simple Annual Interest

Suppose the creditor lends the borrower $1,000 for one year at 10% interest. At the end of the year the borrower repays the lender $1,100. That is simple annual interest and the APR is 10%.

Add-On Interest

In this case, which is the usual method of charging for extending credit, the 10% or $100 charged for the $1,000 loan, is added on to the principal sum at the outset. Then the borrower has to repay the $1,100 in twelve monthly installments of $91.67 and the APR is 18.5% (which is the interest figure that must be quoted to the borrower rather than quoting 10%). Under the add-on method, the borrower has the full use of the $1,000 during the first month only. Thereafter, he or she has decreasing use of the $1,000 as follows: 11/12ths, 10/12ths, 9/12ths, etc. until the final month when he or she has use of only 1/12th of the $1,000. In effect, the borrower is paying a $100 rental fee but does not have all of the money all of the time as he or she would if he or she were paying simple annual interest; or paying the interest only at the beginning of the loan period or throughout the year; or at the end of the loan period when the principal is repaid in one lump sum.

Discount Interest

If the same $1,000 was borrowed on a discount basis, the $100 would be deducted immediately from the principal and the borrower would receive $900. In such a case, the 10% simple interest would translate into an APR of 20.5% (again, this figure must be quoted to the borrower) and the borrower would have an average of only $487.50 at his or her disposal during the course of the year.

Interest on the Unpaid Balance

The usual method used to compute interest on open-end loans is to charge a flat daily or monthly rate on the unpaid balance. Thus, if a flat monthly rate of 1½% is established (and if permitted by law), the daily rate is .04931% and the APR is 18%.

What Interest Rate to Charge

If it is the intention of the lender to charge different rates of interest for different types of loans (which usually is the case), the written lending policy must spell out the classification of loans and the rates to be charged for each. Classifications should be based on the types of credit lines or loan plans offered, the purpose of each loan, and the type or value of any security that may be required in relation to the extent of credit being granted. For example, a lender might establish as one loan classification: "unsecured, closed-end, monthly-payment, signature loan" that bears an 18% annual percentage rate. A second classification might be: "closed-end, monthly-payment, new automobile loan not to exceed 80% of the value of the automobile" at a variable interest rate. There are, of course, no restrictions on the number of reasonable loan classifications a lender might set up, providing each offers the same interest rate for all borrowers and each has the same criteria applied uniformly to all borrowers.

Five Basic Factors for Establishing Lending Criteria

In review, the policy makers for the lending institution should consider five basic factors when establishing the lending criteria.

These are: 1. the borrower's income to be used to repay the loan; 2. the applicant's financial needs and commitments; 3. other valid factors of credit worthiness as determined by the policy makers; 4. the best interests of both the lender and the borrower; 5. evidence of the financial responsibility of any endorser including the endorser's past borrowing history and the value that must be possessed by any security required to grant the loan.

TABLE 3–1   Interest Income and Annual Percentage Rate Comparisons (Return on lending $1,000 for 1 year repaid in 12 monthly payments.)

Annual Add-on Rate (cannot be quoted to borrower)	Add-on *Annual Percentage Rate (must be quoted to borrower)*	*Annual Interest Income*
6%	11.1%	$60.00
7	12.9	70.00
8	14.8	80.00
9	16.6	90.00
10	18.5	100.00
11	20.3	110.00
12	22.2	120.00
13	24.0	130.00
14	25.9	140.00
15	27.7	150.00
16	29.5	160.00
17	31.4	170.00
18	33.2	180.00

Annual Discount Rate (cannot be quoted to customer)	Discount *Annual Percentage Rate (must be quoted to customer)*	*Annual Interest Income*
6%	11.8%	$63.80
7	13.9	75.30
8	16.1	87.00
9	18.3	98.90
10	20.5	111.10
11	22.8	123.60

	Discount	
Annual Discount Rate (cannot be quoted to customer)	Annual Percentage Rate (must be quoted to customer)	Annual Interest Income
12	25.2	136.40
13	27.6	149.40
14	30.1	162.80
15	32.6	176.50
16	35.2	190.50
17	37.8	204.80
18	40.5	219.50

	Unpaid Balance	
Monthly Rate	Annual Percentage Rate	Annual Interest Income
1%	12.0%	$65.00
1½	18.0	97.50
2	24.0	130.00
2½	30.0	162.50
3	36.0	195.00

Finance and/or Service Charges

Truth-in-Lending laws require that any fees or service charges that might be attached to a loan must be calculated into the APR and revealed to the borrower, with certain exceptions. If there is a loan application fee (and these are becoming more common), it must be included in the APR. However, if the fee is charged only if the application is rejected (to cover the cost of processing it), or the fee is returned if the loan is approved, then it does not have to be disclosed. If there is a charge for insurance, this can be noted separately on the disclosure statement and does not have to be included in the APR. Late charges also do not have to be calculated into the APR but the method of calculation must be disclosed to the borrower at the time the note is executed.

Loan Payments

Regardless of the type of loans the lender may decide to offer, there are three basic approaches to loan payments. These are: 1.

equal payments of interest with each payment of principal; 2. payment of interest with principal to be paid at some future date; 3. payment of principal and interest through the scheduling of required loan payments in a manner that will insure payment of the loan in full at maturity.

As part of the lending policies and procedures, the loan repayment methods must be determined. Rules concerning the intervals between loan payments should be specific. A single-payment loan requires a specific maturity date and should provide for the annual payment of interest even though the principal balance may be due on one specific date. Education loans offer a degree of payment flexibility not found in other types of consumer loans in that repayment can be deferred until schooling is completed or interest alone may be paid with principal deferred for a substantial period of time. For all other types of loans—except lines of credit—there should be substantial equal payments of principal and interest (unless paid in advance) throughout the life of the loan.

Lines of Credit

A line of credit loan is different from other consumer loans in that the amount of credit available to the borrower is automatically replenished as payments are made. For example, if an individual has a $5,000 line of credit, he or she may borrow and repay that amount repeatedly without having to reapply for each new borrowing. Usually, a line of credit loan policy requires that payments be made at least once a month. However, a "pay-interest-only for-a-month" feature or a "skip-a-payment" feature gives the borrower the opportunity to miss one or more monthly payments annually (usually during a period when consumer spending is heavy, such as Christmas) while permitting the lender to extend the life of the loan and the interest income due. If this is done, it must conform to credit laws.

The following conditions should be included in the line of credit policy: 1. the credit limit available; 2. the required monthly payments; 3. the interest rate and service charges; 4. the borrower's promise to repay; 5. the ability of the borrower to repay on any business day without penalty; 6. the ability of the lender to terminate the agreement under specified circumstances; 7. the ability of the lender to increase or decrease the interest rate on further advances after giving proper notice; 8. any other conditions that the policy maker wishes to incorporate to protect the lender and to comply with existing laws and regulations.

Because the line-of-credit loan can be continually renewed by the borrower, the lender should establish a review policy and determine to reexamine each borrower's loan file on some regular basis—at least every 24 to 36 months. The purpose of such a review is to obtain current information that is needed to reassess the borrower's credit worthiness. The date of such a review should be documented in the customer's loan file and a new loan application may or may not be required at that time depending on the lender's policies regarding open-end credit.

If the line of credit is terminated, written notice of the termination should be sent to the borrower. Obviously, such a termination does not negate the borrower's obligation to repay any outstanding loan balance that might exist.

If the lender desires either to increase the customer's credit line or to extend the payment terms beyond the original period, a new application should be received.

The lender should also establish a policy regarding control of the advances over and above the authorized line of credit. Such a policy might call for immediate contact of the borrower by telephone, the refusal to grant any further requests for loans until the borrower has repaid the excess advance, a procedure for transferring money from a savings or checking account to cover the excess amount of the loan, or an increase in interest rates charged.

Loans to "Insiders"—Employees or Officers

Every lender should establish a policy about granting loans to its officers or employees. If the policy permits such loans, a procedure should be set up for appointing one or more individuals to be responsible for making certain that the loan applications are complete as to income and debt obligations and that the responsibility for approving all applications is clearly assigned and the established procedures are followed. No insider should ever be given the privilege of approving his or her own loan application.

When making loans to insiders, the lender might wish to offer an interest rate that is lower than the rate granted to other borrowers (an "employee discount"). This is a fairly common practice but, such a policy must be applied equally to all officers and employees and *must conform to existing laws.*

Guidelines for Establishing Lending and Collecting Policies and Procedures

When a lender establishes both his or her credit policies and the procedures to be followed, there are certain well-established guidelines that should be followed. These include:

1. All policies and procedures should be put into writing. Verbal policies and procedures should not be tolerated because they lead to misunderstanding and abuse.
2. A policy and procedure committee of select officers and employees of the lending institution (including the individual responsible for managing the retail credit operations) should be established to review and change existing policies and procedures when necessary and to create new ones if required.
3. The committee should be small enough so it is not unwieldly and should be given the necessary authority to implement the lending policies and procedures it creates. Care should be taken that the committee members are chosen so they reflect the best interests of the lending institution as a whole rather than those of an individual or special interest group. For example, the board of directors or the chief executive officer should not be given sole authority. Credit policies and procedures should be established without bias or prejudice.
4. Initially, the committee should draft a temporary policy based on:
   • An analysis of delinquents if the lender has previous retail lending activity.
   • A random selection of lending and collecting policies and procedures used by other lenders. Because these are usually created as a matter of public record, they are not difficult to obtain by requesting them from other consumer credit grantors. (See figure 3–3 Consumer Credit Policy Outline.)

FIGURE 3–3   Consumer Credit Policy Outline

1. General Policy Statement
2. Lending Authority (Who is authorized to extend credit and under what circumstances.)
3. Types of Credit Offered
   a. Personal installment loans
   b. Automobile loans
   c. Secured loans
   d. Home improvement loans
   e. Revolving credit
   f. Education loans
   g. Other
4. Interest Rates and Terms
5. Underwriting Guidelines
   A. Policy concerning applicants
      a. Application
      b. Income from all sources
      c. Employment
      d. Minimum age
      e. Residence
      f. Capacity to repay
      g. Credit history
      h. Telephone
      i. Co-signers
      j. Disputes
   B. Policy concerning types of loans offered
6. Collection Guidelines
   A. Policy concerning delinquent loans
      a. How and when various procedures engaged
      b. Permissable collection methods

5. The procedures instituted by the committee should be as simple and uncomplicated as possible. And they should include both the manual and automated steps to be followed when processing and collecting all types of loans offered by the lender. No two lenders' procedures will be exactly alike. They will have their own peculiarities and preferences—whether it's the hours during which consumer credit information will be provided to other lenders, the color-coding of various forms, or the place or manner in which loan interviews are to be conducted. Therefore, every committee

should custom-make its own consumer credit procedures and not slavishly follow those of another.

6. Having established temporary credit policies and procedures, the committee should put them into practice during a test period. This should be a time when every policy and procedure is given adequate time and use to determine if it is desirable and practical. If one is found to be wanting, unworkable, or unnecessary, the committee should either revise it or discard it.

7. Following the testing period during which the policies and procedures are honed, the final version should be endorsed or ratified in writing by the governing body of the lending agency (which will probably be either the board of directors or the general partners).

8. Finally, the committee should establish a system which insures that the policies and procedures are not cast in stone but can be updated and kept in compliance with any future federal or state regulations which may be created, or future operational changes which may dictate revisions in the policies and procedures.

4

Typical Consumer Credit Department Lending Policy and Procedures

---

GENERAL POLICY STATEMENTS

Consumer Lending Policy

It is part of the overall stated corporate objectives of (lender) concerning the investment of available funds, to first satisfy the consumer credit needs of qualified borrowers in our service area at competitive rates of interest and on a non-discriminatory basis. It is to accomplish this purpose that the following guidelines are set forth.

Consumer Lending Goals

From time to time and at least annually, the Consumer Credit Department should survey the immediate competition and establish objectives for both volume and yield for each type of consumer loan offered. In addition, special programs may be initiated from time to time to increase our penetration of certain consumer loan markets. These objectives shall be set forth at least annually in a written plan for the forthcoming year. The attainment of these objectives shall be the responsibility of the head of the Consumer Credit Department.

Consumer Credit Underwriting Guidelines

It is the policy of_____to extend credit in accordance with written underwriting guidelines and with any local, state, or national laws regulating consumer credit. These laws and guidelines set forth policy concerning applicants and concerning the various types of loans offered. The head of the Consumer Credit Department is responsible for seeing that all laws and guidelines are followed by the employees of_____and it is his or her responsibility to initiate any additions or changes that may be necessary. These shall be approved by the Chief Executive Officer and the Board of Directors prior to becoming effective.

Consumer Credit Policy Objectives

Following are the overall objectives of the consumer credit policy of_____:

1. The credit policy of_____is based first on safety of principal and, second, on creating earnings compatible with the investment of principal. The availability of funds and the ratio of investments of various types must always be a governing factor.
2. Credit is to be extended to those individuals who fulfill the requirements listed in this manual.
3. Credit is to be offered in order to retain existing business and to develop new business for_____in the form of savings and investment accounts, loans, financial planning, and other financial services.
4. The Equal Credit Opportunity Act and its Revised Regulation B shall be adhered to in all credit transactions. These provide (among other things) that it shall be unlawful to

discriminate in applications for consumer credit for the following reasons:
a. Sex
b. Marital status
c. Race
d. Color
e. Creed
f. National origin
g. Age (providing the applicant has the legal capacity to enter into a binding contract)
h. Because the applicant receives public assistance
i. Because the applicant has exercised his or her rights under the Consumers' Credit Act
j. Because the applicant deals with persons of a particular race, color, religion, national origin, sex, marital status, or age

Consumer Loan Rates and Terms

Consumer loan rates and terms offered by _____ to qualified applicants shall be set forth from time to time in an updated "Interest Rate and Terms" chart which is part of the Consumer Lending Policy. It shall be available to all employees and to all loan applicants. The Consumer Loan Rate Chart shall be maintained on a current basis at all time by the head of the Consumer Credit Department and shall be approved by the Chief Executive Officer prior to becoming effective. Interest rates and loan terms are granted on a completely non-discriminatory basis to all applicants who qualify for credit under existing laws and the underwriting guidelines. (See table 4-1)

Credit Authorizations

Credit authorization powers are approved and extended by the Board of Directors on the recommendation of the Chief Executive Officer. The decision to authorize or decline credit is at the discretion only of those so authorized. Decisions may be overridden only by the Board of Directors. It is the policy of _____ that credit decisions are made by individuals with credit authorization in accordance with the established Underwriting Policy and further that said individuals stay fully informed as to this policy and the laws which also govern it.

Approvals, Declines, and Changes

Approvals, declines, and changes shall be made in written form in all cases. Oral notices may be given at the request of the customer but must be acknowledged in writing after the fact.

TYPES OF CREDIT OFFERED

Personal Unsecured Installment Loans

A. Description:
   A loan of this type, with or without security, provides cash or credit to the applicant with principal and add-on simple interest usually divided into equal monthly payments over a specified term.
B. Purpose:
   The proceeds may be used for any legitimate legal activity.
C. Security:
   _____ relies solely on the character, capability, capacity, and credit record of the applicant, as well as its own past experience.
D. Loan Limit:
   The maximum loan in this category to any individual is $_____ .
E. Terms and Rates:
   The maximum term on this type of loan is _____ months unless otherwise extended by a senior officer. The interest rate is to be determined according to the current rate chart included in this manual.
F. Forms:
   The forms required to complete this type of loan are:
   1. A completed and signed application by the maker of the note with a credit check. If the applicant is self-employed, a current financial statement or the most recent tax return should accompany the application. If there is a comaker, the same forms are required.
   2. A completed and signed three-(3) part note.
   3. An adverse action report is needed if the application is rejected.
   4. If a counter offer is made, a form is needed to inform the applicant of the new offer.

Collateral Demand Loans (Secured)

A. Description:

    _____offers two types of collateral demand loans. A passbook loan is a collateral loan fully secured by a savings account passbook from this institution and the loan is written payable on demand. An "other securities" loan is a loan fully secured by a savings passbook from another financial institution, by listed stocks, transferable bonds, or the cash surrender value of life insurance. It is payable on demand.

B. Purpose:

Such a loan may be taken for any reason. The purpose need not be revealed nor are credit references required except as required by Federal Regulations concerning the carrying of securities (Regulation U).

C. Security:

A savings passbook is held by_____and a hold on the account is placed in the computer with an automatic stop placed on withdrawals. If the passbook is from another institution, the loan officer must verify by telephone and in writing with the issuing institution that the passbook is not lost, stolen, or pledged towards another loan. The other institution also must be notified in writing when the loan is paid and the collateral released. It is the responsibility of the approving loan officer to verify the positive identification of the borrower on all passbooks and other secured loans. Notification must be given to the issuer of either pledged passbooks or life insurance policies that such items are assigned. Pledged passbooks must be accompanied by a properly executed withdrawal form and pledged stocks, bonds, and insurance by valid powers of assumption. Acknowledgements of the assignments should be secured along with passbooks, stocks, bonds, life insurance policies, assignment forms, and withdrawal orders which are kept in a secured place for the duration of the loan.

D. Loan Limit:

The policy of_____is to limit the amount of a passbook loan to ____% of the passbook balance. "Other Securities" loans are limited as follows:

* ____% of stock or bond value traded on the New York Stock Exchange

    * ____ % of all other stock and bond value
    * ____ % of U.S. Government or Federal Agency bonds
    *NOTE—if stock was purchased on margin, check current
    federal regulations for % of stock value.

E. Terms and Rates:

    There is no term on this type of loan and reduction of the
    principal is not mandatory. The debtor is required to pay
    interest quarterly according to the current rate chart included
    in this manual.

F. Forms:

    The forms required to complete this type of loan are:

    Passbook Loan

    1. Three-part collateral loan note with attached withdrawal
        form.
    2. Collateral control card.

    Other Securities

    1. Three-part collateral loan note.
    2. Negotiable instrument assigment form.
    3. Federal Reserve Form U-1 on all stock-secured loans.
    4. Passbook on other institutions.
        a. Notice of Assignment of Account form to be sent to other
            institution. Release form to be retained.
        b. Signed withdrawal slip.

LOAN ORIGINATION

Application and Signatures

Regulation B defines application as an oral or written request
for an extension or credit that is made in accordance with procedures
established by a creditor for the type of credit requested. There are
three methods of completing an application:

1. Have the applicant complete the application in the presence
    of the loan officer, and have the loan officer later review the
    application with the applicant.
2. Have the loan officer complete the application with the
    applicant present. (Loan officer must give "Other Income"
    ECOA warning.)

3. Give or mail the application to the applicant to complete in the privacy of his or her choosing, or complete a telephone application.

The first method is workable for large departments with a steady stream of applicants. The problem with having the applicant fill out his or her own application is legibility and comprehensiveness. It is vital for the loan officer to *review all the information carefully* to be sure all the appropriate spaces are filled in and legible.

The second method is the best all around procedure in terms of establishing a customer-bank relationship and getting the application filled in completely and properly with the officer giving the ECOA warning.

The third method is inadequate in terms of encouraging an applicant's new loan business since it is impersonal and time consuming. However, in some cases the applicant may request this method.

Applications may be taken over the telephone when personal interviews are not possible or practical. Do not lose business to competitors offering this type of loan service. Obviously, if the loan officer requested is with another applicant, the phone applicant should be transferred to another loan officer, or a call-back message taken and followed up.

Complete applications should be on file for each applicant obligated on a loan with the understanding that credit references are to be reported under all signatures listed on the note, unless otherwise requested by the applicants so obligated. Documents relating to a loan closing (i.e., application, note, etc.) may only be completed and signed outside the loan office when signatures of the applicants are on file.

With established customers, loans may be completed by mail if the applicant requests. If approved, the note and necessary papers should be typed and sent without delay to the customer with a stamped return envelope. When the signed papers are returned, the check may be sent out. If it is a joint loan, the check should be made payable to both parties.

All parties to the loan should be present in the loan office when loans made to new applicants are closed. Proper identification of all parties should be obtained before the loan is consummated. This is an important point because many times care in identifying new applicants is lacking. The identification process should be the same for new loans as it is for cashing checks for unknown customers. *Be very careful!*

Generally, the loan proceeds are far in excess of any check that will be cashed over the counter. If the applicant cannot identify himself or herself, do not pay the loan out until proper identification is provided.

Studies of past loan losses indicate that if complete information had been required and obtained at the time of the application, the loan would not have been granted, and a loss would not have occurred. *Get a complete application on all loans, both new and rewrites!*

Interviewing

A credit interview has three purposes:

1. To *obtain* sufficient information about the applicant to allow an informed and intelligent decision on the application.
2. To *provide* information to the applicant about credit terms and policies, and to stress the effect of prompt payment in establishing and maintaining a good credit record.
3. To *sell* the applicant on other loan services and to cross-sell other services.

Interviewing style is a personal trait and will vary with the personality and experience of the loan officer. However, the following points should be common to all interviews:

1. Treat applicants as you want to be treated. Don't keep them waiting at a desk or waiting for a return phone call.
2. Rise and introduce yourself to each applicant with a sincere, firm friendly handshake and a smile. Remember, good customers develop from properly treated applicants who pay operating expenses including salaries.
3. Put the applicant at ease through a brief casual conversation or a pleasant "How may we help you?"
4. Ask questions that require a descriptive answer, "You don't have any other loans, do you?"

5. Allow the applicant time to answer, especially when inquiring about *obligations*. Remember, get as complete a credit history as possible.
6. Pay strict attention to the applicant during the interview. This is courteous as well as prudent since you may observe something that will prompt you to inquire further into a particular topic.
7. Make the applicant realize that she or he is very important to you, the loan officer, and the lending institution.

To insure compliance with the Federal Equal Credit Opportunity Act (ECOA) regulations, the following in the areas of applications will be the lender's policy.

Transactions Relating to Requests for Loans by Individuals

You may not make any oral or written statements to an applicant or prospective applicant concerning the following that would discourage that person from submitting or completing an application or financial statement: (a) race; (b) color; (c) religion; (d) national origin; (e) sex; (f) marital status; (g) age; (h) receipt of income from a public assistance program; or (i) the good faith exercise of rights under the Consumer Credit Protection Act. For example, you may not say to a married woman who applies for individual credit that it is the lender's policy to require her husband to cosign the note. You must also avoid any condescending statements, however casual, such as a statement to a femal applicant who is applying for a loan that "you don't have to worry about the loan; in the end it will be your husband's obligation anyway." This is not a fact, only those who sign are liable.

In many situations, an applicant for credit will discuss the request for credit and provide you with a completed application, financial statement, and other supporting documentation which you may request, such as income tax returns, or you will sit down with the applicant and assist in completing the application and financial statement and review the supporting documentation which the application has provided.

The following are factors which you should consider in reviewing or completing the applicant's application, financial statement and supporting documentation.

1.   You may not request an applicant's sex or marital status in connection with any application.

2.   If two people apply jointly for a loan, you may not inquire about their relationship to one another.

   A.   You may not request any information about the applicant's spouse, unless the spouse is a joint applicant. Under Regulation B the following are among the exceptions to the prohibition that enables the creditor to request information concerning the applicant's spouse:

      a.   where the applicant is relying on the spouse's income as a basis for repayment; and

      b.   where the applicant resides in a community property state or property upon which the applicant is relying as a basis for repayment of the credit requested is located in such a state.

   Note: The spouse is a joint applicant: (1) when he or she is indicated as such on the application, or (2) if he or she is indicated as a joint applicant in response to a question regarding who is applying for the loan. In the case of an oral response, you should note who indicated the joint application, and the date, for your files.

3.   You may not request an applicant's race, color, religion, or national origin.

4.   If an applicant lists on the application or financial statement (or if such information is listed in any supporting documentation such as income tax returns) *income* derived from a *public assistance program*, you may request that the applicant provide verification of the *amount and regularity of payments*. This is permissable only when the income is a relevant factor in the credit decision. Under no circumstances may you discuss a public assistance program for any other reason.

5.   Before you can ask for any information regarding alimony, child support, or separate maintenance payments, the applicant must be advised by insertion of the information on the application, that applicants need not list income derived from alimony, child

support, or separate maintenace payments unless they wish to have such income considered in the credit determination or ability to repay the loan. If an applicant indicates on the application or financial statement that a source of his or her income is from *alimony, child support*, or *separate maintenance* payments on the application or financial statement, you may request that the applicant provide verification of the *amount and regularity of payments*. This is permissable only when the income is a relevant factor in the credit decision or ability to repay the loan.

6.   If you determine from the information supplied by an applicant that the applicant does not qualify for credit in the amount or on the terms requested, you may suggest that the applicant offer additional collateral or obtain a cosigner or guarantor for the loan. *You may not suggest, however, that the applicant's spouse be the one to provide the collateral.* You should maintain a written record of any suggestions regarding additional collateral or obtaining a cosigner or guarantor made to an applicant along with the duplicates of all other written information pertaining to the loan application including the application, financial statement, and other supporting documentation for the loan.

7.   If you inform an applicant that the lender does not offer the type of credit requested (for example, if the applicant requested a bank charge card that the lender does not offer), you should record this fact along with your explanation and any inquiries which the applicant may make in response.

8.   If you receive an incomplete application or if the financial statement or supporting documentation does not contain all the information requested, you must make a reasonable effort to obtain the information that has been omitted. If the applicant provides this information by telephone, you should record the information on a supplemental document and attach it to the original application. You should never return any of the original documentation to the applicant. You must be sure that the information, especially numerical figures received during a telephone conversation, is recorded accurately. If you send the applicant a new application to be completed, you must indicate what information is needed and that the new application is supplementary and will be attached to the original documentation when returned. If the applicant does not return the supplementary application within 30 days, the application is considered denied.

9.   You may request an applicant to list all accounts for which he or she is liable and to provide the name and address in which each such account is maintained. You may also ask for all names, including "d/b/a's," in which the applicant has previously received credit.

10.   A creditor shall request an applicant's *race/national origin, sex, and marital status* as required in *section 13* of Regulation B (*information for monitoring purposes*). In addition, a creditor may obtain such information as may be required by a regulation, order, or agreement, issued by, or entered into with a court or an enforcement agency (including the Attorney General of the United States or a similar state official) to monitor or enforce compliance with any credit discrimination statute, this regulation, or other federal or state statute or regulation.

Such monitoring information is presently required;

1. in some loans for owner occupied purchase of an existing dwelling place and

2. for loans under the Guaranteed Student Loan Program as per the HELP approved application.

Note: The consumer may choose *not* to answer the monitoring section and should indicate his or her choice in writing.

Specific Credit Standards and Limitations

The following specific limitations are to be followed as policy:

Geographic Loan Area—An applicant (defined as a person who requests, or who has received an extension of credit) must either *work, live,* or *own property* in the geographic land area commonly described and known as _____.

Minimum Loan Limit—Due to the cost of setting up and maintaining an installment loan, the minimum amount of an installment loan will be $_____.

Length of Residency in Lending Area—_____ months residency in _____ lending area will be viewed as necessary for approval (with reasonable exceptions).

Length of Employment—_____ months steady employment with a single employer will be viewed as necessary for approval (optional).

Disposable Income Percentage for Monthly Payments—_____% to _____% of the net disposable income will be viewed as reasonable percentage for total monthly payments excluding food, housing, and utilities (optional).

Officer's Approval—Any loan application with proceeds in excess of $____ or a re-written loan with a balance of over $____ shall be reviewed and initialled by at least_____ loan officers before approval and disbursement.

Rewritten Loans—An installment loan must be repaid a minimum of ____months, or _____% of the term of the loan, or _____ the original dollar amount before eligible to be rewritten.

Charge-Off/Bankruptcy—A loan may not be extended to an applicant who has an unrecovered charged-off loan with _____ or any other lender, or has been declared a bankrupt within the past ten years.

Relatives/Business/Personal/Employees and Families—No loan officer shall either accept an application, approve, process, or disburse funds to a loan applicant seeking an unsecured loan who is a relative, or in any other case where the loan officer's judgment would be unduly influenced as a result of any known past, present, or future business or personal relationship with that applicant. Loans shall not be made to employees or their immediate families (father, mothers, brothers, sisters, sons, daughters).

Credit and Approval

All credit applications will be sent to the credit department for credit verification.

Credit verification should be done in a neat, orderly, legible, prompt manner.

Care and completeness must be the byword. This is the first level of delinquency prevention and the opportunity to screen applicants who may develop into collection problems and loan losses, and is the principal reason for a credit checking function.

Normally credit will be verified on all applications on the same day they are received by the credit department. Rush applications accepted at branches may be phoned in to the credit department if the customer requests same day approval.

Delays on applications are usually caused by incomplete or inadequate information on the application. Therefore, it is imperative that all applications be *complete* and *legible* including accounts and telephone numbers, balances, and payment amounts.

Credit Checking Procedure

1.   Ensure that the application is *dated* and *signed* by the applicant.

2.   Review the application completely *before* beginning the credit check to ensure sufficient information to proceed.

3.   Check all office files to determine if applicant is listed as present customer, previous customer, or a previous turn-down or charge-off. This step is vital and should be done *before any other verifications are made*. It could save considerable time and money.

4.   Verify current residence address and employment. In the case of rental residence landlords should be called; and city directory's, telephone books, and bank mortgage files checked for owner-occupied residences. When speaking to a personnel department or whenever it is possible, verify the fact of employment, as well as the starting date, position and salary of the applicant.

5.   It is_____'s policy to *clear all* applicant's credit with the appropriate local *credit bureau* by requesting a phone record to be recorded and initialed and included in applicant's file, or by initiating a computerized printout of an applicant's credit history from a credit bureau. This credit clearing is required of all new applicants, all previous borrowers, and all rewrites as well as re-checks on any accounts which go _____ days or more past-due as an aid in collection procedures.

Particular attention should be paid to the *date of the file information, recent inquiries, the trade reporting date if it is different from the credit check date, and derogatory information—including collection—if any*. If this information is not given, ask for it. If there is none, write "none" in the appropriate section of the credit check. Always ask for all the information on file when making credit bureau checks.

Remember, a credit bureau report showing no derogatory information, may be just as valuable as a report full of collection items and charge-offs. Good loans keep us in business!

Listed references should be checked individually. Attempt to *get facts*, as required by law, and not opinion.

6. In the case of home improvement loans, be certain the property ownership has been verified from mortgage files and a credit update has been obtained.

Good judgment, imagination, persistence, curiosity, and a pleasing telephone personality contribute toward a good credit check—one that is complete, correct, legible, and that will guide the loan officer to a correct loan decision.

When the credit check is completed, the application properly checked and initialled will be returned promptly to the appropriate loan officer for her or his review and decision. Any requested deadline marked on the face of the application will be noted and if unable to meet this, the loan officer will be called. If anything out of the ordinary, or a reason to be cautious is noticed, this will be called to the loan officer's attention as well.

Evaluation of Applications

Transactions Relating to Requests by Individuals for Loans
In evaluating an application for a loan you *may not consider* the *race, color, religion, national origin, sex,* or *marital status* of any person connected in any manner with the credit request.

You may consider an applicant's age only for the purpose of determining a pertinent element of creditworthiness, or to determine if credit life insurance is applicable. For example, you may consider the length of time to retirement and if retirement income will support the loan until maturity. You may also consider an applicant's age in assessing the significance of the applicant's length of employment or residence.

Although you probably seldom encounter a request for a loan by an applicant under ＿＿years old, you may decline a loan if the applicant is under ＿＿years of age and has not reached majority.

With respect to a request by an individual for a loan, you may consider the fact that an applicant's income is derived from a public assistance program only for the purpose of determining a pertinent element of creditworthiness. For example, you may consider the length of time an applicant has been receiving such income, such as VA benefits or disability benefits, and whether the applicant intends to continue to reside in the applicable jurisdiction in relation to the residency requirements for receipt of such public assistance benefits; and you may consider the status of an applicant's dependents to determine whether benefits the applicant is presently receiving will continue. Public assistance programs include any federal, state, or local government assistance program which provides a continuing periodic income supplement, whether based on entitlement or need. The term public assistance program includes, but is not limited to, Aid to Families with Dependent Children, food stamps, rent and mortgage supplemental security income, and unemployment compensation.

You *must consider* income derived from part-time employment, annuity, pension or any other retirement benefits in evaluating an application. In considering such income, you may consider the amount and probable continuance of the income. This includes the length of the annuity or retirement benefit, any changes that may be anticipated in the amount of the benefit, and the applicant's eligibility for the benefit. You may ask for supporting data or other information regarding receipt of such employment, annuity, pension or other retirement benefit income.

If a person requests a loan and lists alimony, child support or separate maintenance payments as income, you *must consider* such payments are likely to be consistently made. Among the factors you may consider in determining the consistency of such income are: whether the payments are received pursuant to a written agreement or court decree, the length of time that the payments have been received, the regularity of receipt of the payments, the availability of procedures to compel payment, and the creditworthiness of the payor. (With respect to the last factor, it should be noted that under the Fair Credit Reporting Act you may not obtain a credit report about an applicant's spouse or former spouse without their written consent.)

When you consider an applicant's credit history in evaluating an application, you must consider any accounts that the applicant and the applicant's spouse are or were permitted to use or for which both are or were contractually liable. You must also consider the credit history of any account reported by the credit bureau in the name of the applicant's spouse or former spouse provided that the applicant is creditworthy. In addition, you must consider any information that the applicant may present which tends to indicate that the credit history being considered *does not accurately* reflect the applicant's creditworthiness.

You may consider whether an applicant is a permanent resident of the United States; the applicant's immigration status; and such additional information as may be necessary to ascertain rights and remedies regarding payment.

You may not take into account the fact that an applicant does not have a telephone listed in his or her name, but you can consider whether there is a phone in the residence of the applicant.

Granting or Denying Credit

Transactions Relating to Requests by Individuals for Loans.

You *may not deny credit* on the basis of *race, color, religion, national origin, sex, marital status, age, receipt of public assistance benefits* or the *good faith exercise of rights under the Consumer Credit Protection Act*. For example, you may not deny an application for credit when you would have granted credit if:

1. The request for the loan had been made by a person of a race different from that of the applicant. For example, if you would have advanced funds to a Caucasian, you should offer to grant credit to an Indian, African, Arab, or Oriental who is substantially similarly situated in all respects other than race.
2. The request for the loan had been made by a person of a color other than that of the applicant. For example, if you would have advanced funds to a white person, you should also offer to grant credit to a red, yellow, black or brown person who could demonstrate that he or she is substantially similarly situated to the white person in all respects other than color.
3. The request for the loan had been made by a person of a religion different from that of the applicant.
4. The request for the loan had been made by a person of a national origin different from that of the applicant. For example, if you would have granted a loan to one of Italian origin, you should offer to grant credit to an applicant who is

of Greek origin if the applicant is substantially similarly situated in all respects other than national origin.

5. The request for the loan had been made by a person of the opposite sex from the applicant. For example, if you would have advanced funds to a male, you should offer to grant credit to a female who is in a substantially similar situation to the male in all respects other than sex.

6. The request for the loan had been made by a married individual rather than an unmarried applicant. If the two people are in substantially similar situtations in all respects other than marital status, you should offer to grant credit to the single person, if you would grant it to the married person.

7. The request for the loan had been made by a salaried person and the applicant receives public assistance benefits such as Aid to Dependent Children. If you would grant credit to the salaried person if he or she requested a substantial install-ment loan and the person on ADC could demonstrate that the public assistance would continue in the same amount as the salaried person's salary and for a length of time sufficient to pay off the loan, you should offer to grant credit to the person receiving ADC.

8. You may not prohibit an applicant from opening or main-taining an account in the applicant's birth-given name and a surname that is the applicant's birth-given surname, or a combined surname, or other regularly used name (AKA).

Transactions Relating to Existing Loan Accounts

It is important to note that Regulation B's Discriminatory pro-scriptions apply not only to an applicant's initial request for exten-sion of business or commercial credit, but also to an existing account's request for an extension of the term, or an increase in the line of credit extended and to the termination of an account or an unfavorable change in the term of an account by the lender that does not affect all or a substantial portion of a particular classification of the lender's accounts.

Thus, for example, if the lender were to terminate a loan because of the principal's divorce or separation or refuse to grant an increase in the borrower's line of credit because of a divorce or separation, it will be engaging in conduct violation of Regulation B.

Also, you may not require a reapplication, change the terms of an account or terminate the account because an applicant who is contractually liable on an existing open-end account has reached a certain age or is retiring, or because of a change in the applicant's name or marital status unless you have evidence of inability or unwillingess on the part of the applicant to repay. However, you may require reapplication with respect to an open-end account if there is a change in the applicant's marital status where the initial credit granted was based on income earned by the applicant's spouse or former spouse, and the applicant's income alone at the time of the original application did not support the amount of credit currently extended.

Individual and Comaker Signature Requirements

Transactions Relating to Requests for Loans by Individual Application for Individual Credit
1. If a person applies for individual credit, whether secured or unsecured, and the applicant's own income and the assets which are in his or her name alone are sufficient for the applicant to qualify for the credit requested, *you may not require the signature of any other person—including the applicant's spouse*—on any loan document, including the note and any other instruments creating the obligation.
2. If a person applies for individual credit, whether secured or unsecured, and the applicant's own income and the assets which are in his or her name alone are *not* sufficient for the applicant to qualify for the credit requested, you may require additional security and/or an endorser.

Closing the Loan

The loan closing may be the last personal contact the borrower has with the loan officer for some time. The borrower's impression of you and the way you close the loan may determine whether or not the applicant returns for a later loan or uses other services, or more importantly, whether he or she recommends _____ to her or his friends and relatives.

Under _____ billing system, an applicant may have a *due* date of the *5th, 10th, 15th, 20th, 25th,* and *30th* of each month. The applicant is allowed to *choose his or her own date* with respect to pay days and other obligations. The applicant must be given at least thirty (30) days for the first payment. Do not arbitrarily choose a date without asking the applicant if it is convenient. An applicant may be given as long as ninety days for the first payment. However, this is immaterial if the final due date is not convenient and condu-cive to prompt payment.

When rewriting a loan, try to keep the same due date as the original if at all possible, mainly because the applicant already has the payment due-date noted in his or her budget. In this way, little or no change in budget planning will be necessary. Do this only after you have rechecked with the applicant about the convenience of the due date. Remember, a convenient due date is the first step toward a promptly repaid loan and a good return customer.

Some things to remember when setting a due date:

1. Customer's pay days or other income dates.
2. Other loans or payments (especially mortgage payments and/or rent payment date).
3. Previous loans with _____.
4. The day the loan is to be paid, remembering that the cus-tomer must be given a minimum of 30 days for the first payment.

A *proper closing* will accomplish three purposes:

1. It will provide the applicant with the needed proceeds in a prompt, courteous, fair, and equal manner.
2. It will lay the ground work for prompt repayment and complete understanding of loan limits. *There are no days of grace.* There is a period of time after which late charges will be assessed. All payments are due on due dates.
3. It will establish _____ as the place to come for future financial needs.

A loan closing should be very positive. You are dealing with an approved borrower and an individual you hope will do additional business with _____. The following points must be covered at the loan closing. The interviewer's style will dictate the manner in which they are handled.

1. Establish rapport by thanking the applicant for his or her business, and making a favorable comment about the purposes of the loan.
2. Allow the customer to read all the figures and contents of the note and go over these with the applicant, making sure the customer receives a copy of both the note and the Errors and Ommissions Law which gives borrowers the opportunity to reconsider and protects them against the lender's oversights or omissions in the contract.
3. Stress the interest rate, due date, and late charge provisions. Review other services with each applicant—this is a cross-selling opportunity not to be overlooked.

Notifying Applicants of Credit Decision and Adverse Action

Transactions Relating to Loans Primarily for Consumer Purposes

1. *Approval*
    You must notify an applicant of the approval of a credit request within____days after receiving a completed application. Frequently a consumer applies at more than one lending institution at one time. Prompt follow-up approvals may mean that _____ gets the loan, while conforming with the law. If you hand deliver or send the customer money or a bank check, you do not have to send a letter of approval, since approval is implicit.

2. *Rejecting the Applicant*
    The first maxim the interviewer must learn is that some applicants should *not* be approved. One applicant with evidence of inability and/or willingness to repay presents greater risk than any lender should accept.
    All applicants can be divided into three general categories as far as creditworthiness is concerned:

1. Definite approval
2. Marginal
3. Decline

The test of a skilled interviewer lies in her or his ability to distinguish between *marginal* and *decline* applicants.

A marginal applicant may be made acceptable by altering the terms of the request, e.g., obtain a comaker, ask for collateral, or decrease loan amount or term requested. This is considered a counter offer.

Marginal loans that have been made acceptable often result in loyal customers.

A wise loan officer will decline an applicant who is unable to meet her or his obligations as agreed until the reason for the problem has been removed. To accept a comaker on such a loan, for example, is to impose a hardship on the comaker and subject the lender to a possible loss of good will if collection must be made through the comaker.

For the long term, the best course of action is to reject all unqualified applicants.

In any case take a positive approach in declining a loan application. Look for ways to make the loan acceptable. Allow any applicant, regardless of his or her qualification, to save face. _____ needs all the good customers we can get and circumstances can change for presently unacceptable applications. This is true, for instance, in the case of younger borrowers.

Part of your service should be ongoing attempts to counsel and educate applicants on how they can correct problems that affect their credit. Development of good customers not only helps you but the community as a whole. All lending institutions are responsible, to some degree, for credit counseling.

3. Adverse action

You must notify an applicant regarding any adverse action you take with respect to an application, whether complete or incomplete, with respect to existing accounts. The ECOA prescribed notification must take place within ____ days after receipt of the application, and within ____ days after taking the action regarding an existing account.

Adverse action means a refusal to grant credit in substantially the terms requested by an applicant (including a refusal to grant a request for an increase in an existing credit line), unless you make a counter offer *and* the applicant uses or expressly accepts the credit offer. (See discussion of counter offers below.) Adverse action also occurs when you terminate or unfavorably change the terms of an account for some reason other than delinquency, default or inactivity unless the change in terms is expressly agreed to by the applicant, if the termination or change does not affect all or a substantial portion of the same classification of account.

The following actions, although adverse to the applicant, *do not require* an *ECOA notification*:
(However, it is strongly suggested that adverse action procedure be used on all loans that are declined.)

(1) As previously noted, changes in the terms of an account expressly agreed to by an applicant in any action; (2) forbearance relating to an account taken in connection with the inactivity, default or delinquency as to that account; (3) a refusal to extend credit at a point of sale or loan in connection with the use of an account because of the credit limit set on that account; (4) a refusal to extend credit because the lender does not offer the *type* of credit plan requested; and (5) a counter offer of credit which the applicant uses or accepts.

4. Counter offers

An example of a counter offer is when an applicant requests a certain amount of credit and the lender offers to grant a lesser amount of credit. If the applicant uses the credit or expressly accepts the lesser amount, there is no adverse action for purposes of the Equal Credit Opportunity Act. If the applicant does not accept the lesser amount, adverse action has occurred and the adverse action notice must be sent to the applicant. Another example of a counter offer is a loan request for ____% financing of the purchase of an automobile which the lender is unwilling to approve because its policy only allows ____% financing. If the customer is unwilling to accept the lender's counter offer of ____% financing, the lender must send a notification of adverse action to the applicant.

5. Withdrawn application

Approved applications may be considered withdrawn if it was understood between the lender and the applicant that he or she would inquire about its status. If the applicant does not do so within ____ days after approval it is considered withdrawn. In these situations the applicant is not entitled to any notice, but one is suggested. If no such understanding exists between the lender and the applicant, written notice of approval must be sent to the applicant. In either case, the original completed application is subject to a twenty-five month record retention requirement. In a participation loan request that is declined, each participating lender must see that their individual notice of declination is sent.

6. Notification—to whom

If there is more than one applicant, the notification need only be sent to one of them, but it should be given to the primary applicant if one is readily apparent. If questionable send one to each.

Each applicant who has a loan application rejected must be notified in writing by means of a *Statement of Credit Denial, Termination, or Change* letter completed and signed by the loan officer who accepted the application within ____days of taking adverse action on the completed loan application. The original is to be hand delivered or mailed to the applicant and the copy attached to the original application is to be filed in a *declined application individual file*.

Creditors Life Insurance

Life insurance coverage on installment loans is provided by____and has become standard procedure with most lenders and is sometimes made available to the applicant at no additional charge, although the customer may indirectly be charged by calculating the insurance cost into the interest charge.

The purpose of this insurance is to insure the life of the principal borrower (the person who signs first). Upon the death of the principal borrower, creditor life insurance will pay the loan off, sparing the family or estate an additional burden. The maximum claim under the policy is $____.

On those loans that carry credit life insurance, ECOA and Regulation B do not prohibit you from asking for age, sex, or marital status of an applicant in connection with credit life insurance if required. You may differentiate in the availability, rates, and terms on which credit life insurance is offered. However, you may not deny or terminate credit because credit insurance is not available on the basis of an applicant's age.

Loan Processing

Loan processing may be defined as the steps taken with the loan paperwork from the time the proceeds are disbursed until the loan is shown as an asset on the institution's books.

Specific instructions for entering loan transactions into a computer are contained in the computer manual.

Loan officers are to deliver to the loan department the necessary documents completed and signed. A work flow chart for both origination and servicing can be of great assistance in this area, when determining the number and quality of employees needed.

Loan department personnel are to complete the loan processing including but not limited to the following major elements:

1. Filing the note in a secure place, numerically, by loan type.
2. Filing the supporting documents—application, credit check, disclosure, correspondence, etc. in individual loan files.
3. Requests for credit information and credit inquiries should all be directed to the loan department. The fact that originally all applications are cleared through a credit bureau, further underlines the *importance* of running a *credit bureau check* on *all applicants*, both new and present borrowers, not only to pick up any other indebtedness, but also any other recent credit inquiries on that applicant for possible use by the loan officers in their loan and collection decisions.
4. Creating an alphabetical-numerical cross reference file using a multi-listing index card filed alphabetically and a loan folder filed numerically. These index cards are important during the complete cycle of the loan, including the paid-up procedure.
5. Ordering a payment book and having it sent to the customer.

SERVICING THE LOAN

Once the proceeds have been disbursed, the servicing function begins.

Prior to Disbursement
A review of all required documents should be conducted by someone other than the person who prepared the loan for disburse-

ment. Ideally, there will be a double check of all documents prior to any funds disbursement.

After Disbursement

The completed documents should be sent to the loan department as soon as possible for processing.

Record Retention

Transactions Relating to Consumer Loans

Retain all documentation and correspondence pertaining to a credit application for _____ months after an applicant is notified of the credit decision. This includes the application form, any information used in evaluating the application, any information obtained for monitoring purposes, the notification informing the applicant of the credit decision, the statement of specific reasons for adverse action, and any statements submitted by the applicant alleging a violation of the Equal Credit Opportunity Act. Also, retain copies of all correspondence and memoranda relating to the loan application, along with the application. In the case of approved loans, the records—including application and note copy—are to be retained for _____ months after the loan is paid in full.

Furnishing Credit Information

For every consumer credit account about which _____ will furnish consumer credit information, it must be determined whether the account is one that an applicant's spouse will be permitted to use or upon which both spouses will be contractually liable other than as guarantors, sureties, or endorsers. Such an account must then be designated to reflect the fact of participation by both spouses, though there need not be any distinguishing between participation as a user or as a contractually liable party. Information must also be furnished concerning such accounts to credit reporting agencies in a manner that will enable the agency to provide access to the information in the name of either spouse.

Requesting the marital status of the applicants or any authorized user of the account on an application either for individual or joint credit is not permitted. Thus, to comply with the requirements of federal law, either report *all* authorized users to the Credit Bureau, or send a follow-up letter to the applicant after the decision to grant credit has been made to determine whether two people contractually liable on an account are married. Always report information to credit bureaus in the names of *all* joint applications, or determine by a follow-up letter whether any of the joint applicants are spouses and if so report the information to the credit bureau in both names. _____'s policy is to *report all authorized users or* those *contractually liable* to the Credit Bureau. The proper use of the multi-listing Index Cards, properly cross referenced, will also assist with separation of credit.

If there is an inquiry regarding a particular applicant, information is to be furnished only in the name of the person about whom such information is requested. This means, that in the case of an individual account with a spouse as an authorized user, if an inquiry is received regarding the spouse who is an authorized user, the information must be furnished in the name of the spouse.

Customer Relations

A letter, signed by the loan officer making the loan should be sent to the applicant thanking her or him for the new or continued business.

The payment coupon book will be automatically mailed directly to the applicant unless other directions are given by the applicant at the loan closing.

During the term of the loan, a letter may be sent to the customer acknowledging a good payment record and reminding him or her of other services, perhaps soliciting furthur installment business timely to the season (i.e., Christmas, vacations, home improvement, or taxes). When the loan is paid in full, the paid documents should be returned to the applicant advising her or him of his or her fine credit rating.

It is imperative that loan officers are well informed on lending policies and are able to convey accurate information in a friendly and courteous manner. This attitude can be carried into the area of loan servicing as well, provided it is coupled with a firm servicing policy that is flexible enough to respond to special situations.

Delinquency and Collection:

When a customer becomes delinquent, it presents the lender with one of the most difficult customer relations problems. Delinquency may not intentional, it may be the result of uncontrollable factors such as sickness, death, unexpected expenses, or marital problems. When delinquency occurs, a lender is faced with the difficult problem of collecting the loan and maintaining good customer rapport.

Collection Procedure:

The collection department should have a collection policy that is firm, tactful, compassionate and flexible, and all collection calls should be referred to them for servicing. The collection department will comply with all regulations pertaining to debt collection.

The following notices will be automatically printed by the institution's computer service on delinquent accounts:

> 1st notice _____ days after the due date.
> 2nd notice headed _____ days after the due date. (If this notice includes a late charge, describe.)
> "Partial Payment Advice" any time a payment of less than the total amount due is paid, acknowledging the payment received and noting the balance remaining due.

The following *Collection Time Frames and Actions* are to be the institution's *policy* on delinquent loans:

1. The activation of a delinquent loan into the collection system will be through:
   a. The Late Payment Notice received _____ days after due. At such time the collection card will be activated into the collection system and notice mailed.
   b. The computer overdue report, generated periodically each month, showing all loans _____ days overdue. The collection card will be activated at this point in time.
2. When a loan becomes _____ days overdue, and there is no activity and no mitigating circumstances, loan should be charged off against reserve for bad debts.

Whenever it becomes necessary for the lender to contact a customer because of delinquency, it is important that the collector determine the root causes of the problem, keeping in mind that 99%

of the time, the loan will be paid when the customer gets by the difficult period she or he is experiencing. Remember, when the loan officer granted the loan, she or he felt the applicant would pay it back and unless the institution finds something to the contrary, collection efforts must be based on this factor.

Late charges:

A late charge of ____% of the payment or $____ whichever is the lesser, will be assessed automatically when a loan is paid more than ____ days beyond its due date.

Late charges may only be waived with the approval of a loan officer.

Extension fees/Interest only

This is applicable on justified accounts only and with the approval of the loan officer. The same applies for rewrites, with no cash advance.

Legal action:

Whenever it is determined that a delinquent account is uncollectable by the collection department, (or if no action or contact within ____ days after the payment is due), that account is to be turned over to a collection agency or an attorney. Before charging the loan off, the account should be discussed with the loan officer who approved the loan.

All collection programs must adhere to "Debt Collection Regulations" as they exist now and may become amended.

Regulations

Numerous regulations for the protection of the consumer have been and continue to be promulgated which affect personal loan documentation and lending and collection practices. It is the stated policy of _____ that all consumer credit department and collection department personnel are encouraged to participate to the degree appropriate in carrying out the existing regulations and in assisting in the promulgation of such regulations and in the development of workable consumer regulations which serve the best interests of both the consumer and the lender.

TABLE 4–1 Current Installment Loan Limits and Rates

Type of Loan	Aggregate Lender Limitations	Aggregate Borrower Limitations	A.P.R.
FHA Home improvement Loans	____% of deposits of a financial institution.	$____ Max. ____ yrs. repay as established by FHA	____%
Home improvement loans	____% of deposits of a financial institution.	$____ (per property) Max.____ year repayment	____%
Privately insured home improvement loans		$____ (per property) Max.____ year repayment	____%
Personal loans and over-draft lending without credit card	Up to ____% of the first $____ million in deposits and ____% of deposits in excess of $____ million of a financial institution.	$____	____%
Eduction loans		Subject to current federal regulations $____	____%
Credit cards/overdraft			____%
Collateral loans:			____%
On authorized bonds and notes		____% of the market value	____%
On passbooks		____% of deposits held by a financial institution	____%
On other bonds, notes and shares		____% on the market value of marketable securities and ____% of the market value of non-marketable securities	____%
On life insurance policies	Up to ____% of the deposits of a financial institution	____% of the cash surrender value of policies issued by life insurance companies	____%

It is the policy of _____ that all members of the consumer credit department and the collection department shall consider it a part of their basic job responsibilities to become fully informed and to stay fully informed as to the appropriate consumer lending regulations which affect their area and that such regulations will be observed with serious cooperation. It is also the policy of _____ to regard such regulations as being in the best interest of the consumer, and, to the degree that we serve the consumer's interest, we shall stringently observe these regulations.

Underwriting Guidelines

It is the policy of _____ that all consumer loan applications shall be taken according to the procedures set forth in the procedures manual for consumer credit and collection. This manual sets forth current lending and collection procedures as approved for and practiced by _____, and such procedures shall be followed to the letter. All forms used in both the lending and collecting activities of _____ are also contained in the manual.

Collection Guidelines

It is the policy of _____ that all collection activities shall be carried out according to the state and federal laws that dictate the collection practices which are to be followed by all consumer lenders. These procedures are to be followed explicitly and careful records and documentation are to be maintained. It is to be remembered that all customers who revert to the status of a collection account are to be treated as a valued customer of _____ and every effort is to be expended to assist the customer into reverting back to the status of a borrower in good standing with _____.

The procedures manual for consumer credit and collection details accepted collection methods to be followed and forms and documentation to be used.

5

Putting the Credit Procedures in Place

FORMS AND PROCEDURES

If any one element of the retail lending and collecting system can be considered to be the most important, it is the procedural. Loan losses will quickly exceed the acceptable level if data is not gathered properly and completely, recorded accurately, maintained so it can be easily tracked, and stored so it can be readily retrieved. What this means is that the lender must design and put into place forms and procedures that will accomplish all of the desired purposes. Procedural matters include:

- Greeting the credit applicant
- Gathering the information desired

- Verifying the facts given

- Reviewing all of the information

- Making the credit determination

- Notifying the applicant of the decision

- Creating the customer file

- Paying out or extending the credit

- Tracking the loan repayment

- Contacting the delinquent borrower

- Collecting the money owed

- Closing the customer file

- Reactivating the customer

Each of the procedural matters involves the development and use of detailed forms and records. Unlike the lender of old, because of today's legal requirements and mass market, it is not practical or possible simply to keep track of extended and outstanding credit by the easiest means as did the retailers of old who kept their records in their heads or literally "on the cuff(s)" of their shirts.

Procedures for Lending and Collecting

Once both people and policies have been put into place (or factored into the consumer credit and collection plans), the creditor must invest considerable time and attention in developing the numerous procedures that will be needed. Procedures for retail lending and collecting that need to be created and followed include everything from the optimum location of the physical space to be occupied and the equipment required, to the forms to be used and the record-keeping methods to be employed. While it is to be expected that every business will determine for itself its own particular procedures for both lending and collecting, there are several basics that must be taken into consideration in order to establish the most efficient and profitable consumer credit operation. (See figure 5–1.)

FIGURE 5–1 *Credit Record Keeping*—The procedural forms used in consumer lending.

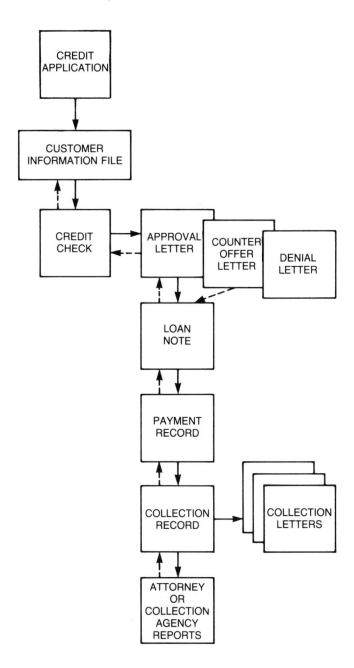

Credit Calls for Privacy

Most borrowers are reticent about broadcasting to the world at large their need to establish credit or borrow money. The typical borrower seeks to make his credit request in private. Therefore, the lender who seeks to encourage credit applications is advised to set up a discreet area (not in the public view) from which to conduct the business of lending and collecting. It is suggested that the lender locate both his credit and collection departments in an area where it is not obvious that a customer is seeking them out. This is the reason so many financial institutions locate their lending operations on a floor separate from the regular banking floor. To set up an obvious "consumer credit" area in full view of the public at large is a mistake that will keep credit business at a minimum.

Greet the Borrower with a Smile

The customer is the heart-blood of every business so the wise retailer makes every effort to extend the warmest welcome possible to every person who comes through her or his door, even when it is the customer's intent to purchase on credit rather than for cash, or it is the customer's desire to borrow money rather than to deposit it. Retail credit customers who repay their debts can be unquestionably the most profitable customers the retailer will ever have. When potential borrowers enter the retail credit department, they should be embraced by a friendly atmosphere conducive to conducting a confidential business transaction with promptness and warmth. The customer should be greeted with a smile by an employee who then determines his or her needs. Depending on the type of credit desired, the applicant should be given the proper application and clear instructions on how to fill it out properly. Then the applicant should be permitted to complete the application in privacy at her or his own pace.

The Forms Needed in the Credit Department

Keeping accurate and up-to-date records is basic to the entire credit operation. These, of course, are gathered on the forms used by the creditor which may be either in hard copy format or computerized depending on the sophistication of the creditor's operations. Suggested forms include: 1. The Credit Application; 2. The

Credit Report; 3. The Disclosure Form; 4. The Loan Note; 5. Payment Reminders; 6. Payment Records; 7. Collection Forms and Records. (See figures 5–2 and 5–3.)

The Credit Application

In putting together his consumer loan operation, Ben put considerable time and effort into the development of a loan application that would provide his loan officers with sufficient data about the borrower to make a realistic decision whether or not to grant credit. (An exception was made for College Book Store members as previously noted in chapter 1, and this exception was the cause of Ben's problems.) A cardinal rule that every lender should follow is that every borrower—regardless of status or position—should complete a loan application, sit through a loan interview, and the credit-worthiness should be judged on the basis of the information provided and gathered and whether or not the applicant meets the lender's guidelines. To make an exception is to create a collection account.

Except for College Book Store members, Ben's approach to the credit application was that at the time individuals apply for credit, they are most willing to give almost any information requested of them and willing to meet almost any reasonable requests made of them in their desire to get an approved loan. For example, on what other occasion could a stranger ask an individual the exact amount of his or her salary or to reveal his or her total debts? A credit applicant is most vulnerable and cooperative while applying for credit. The lender should approach the application with the dual intent of obtaining sufficient data to make a reasonably accurate decision about the applicant's credit worthiness and ability to repay, and to gather additional data that could be used effectively if collection procedures became necessary. It may take the applicant more time to fill out such an application and the creditor more time to conduct the interview and to process the information received, but it will pay dividends to the lender in the long run.

The Purpose of the Application

The purpose of the credit application is to provide the lender with sufficient data so the lender can then make a thorough credit

FIGURE 5–2 *The Credit Steps*—From Application to Action

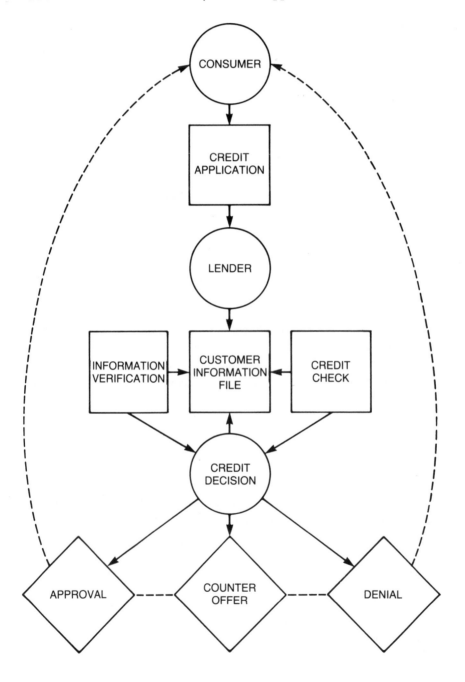

FIGURE 5–3   *The Credit Steps*—From Credit Granting to Repayment

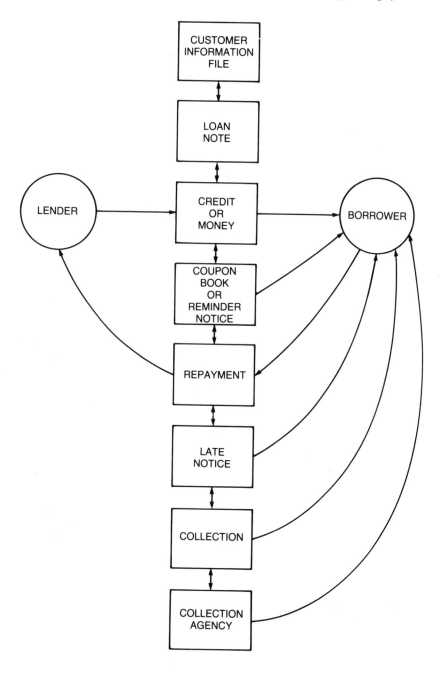

FIGURE 5–4

_____ CREDIT UNION   **CREDIT APPLICATION**

I/We hereby make application individually ☐ or jointly ☐ for a loan of $_____

For a period of _____ months. Purpose of loan _____.

If loan is for a motor vehicle, etc. indicate Year _____ Make _____ Price $_____

NAME	DATE OF BIRTH	SOCIAL SECURITY NO.
ADDRESS STREET TOWN ZIP CODE	HOW LONG?	HOME TELEPHONE

MAILING ADDRESS, IF DIFFERENT:

(If at present address less than 5 years list previous address(es) below.) **PREVIOUS**	HOW LONG?
PREVIOUS	HOW LONG?

NO. OF DEP.	Is applicant liable for alimony, child support or maintenance?	MONTHLY PAYMENT $

Alimony, child support, or separate maintenance income need not be revealed if you do not wish to have it considered as a basis for repaying this obligation.

Does applicant derive income from alimony, child support or maintenance?	MONTHLY INCOME $

(NOTE: SUCH SOURCE OF INCOME NEED NOT BE REVEALED IF APPLICANT CHOOSES NOT TO PROVIDE IT.)

EMPLOYER	HOW LONG?	POSITION
ADDRESS	PHONE	MONTHLY/WEEKLY GROSS INC. $

(If at present employment less than 5 years, list previous employments below.) **PREVIOUS EMPLOYER**	HOW LONG?	POSITION
PREVIOUS EMPLOYER	HOW LONG?	POSITION

SOURCE OF OTHER INCOME FROM SALARY, WAGES OR INVESTMENTS	AMOUNT $

NAME OF BANK HOLDING MORTGAGE ON HOME	ACCOUNT NUMBER	IN WHOSE NAME?
MARKET VALUE $	TAXES CURRENT YEAR $	ORIG. AMT. MORTGAGE $	BALANCE $	PAYMENT $

IF RENTING - NAME OF LANDLORD	MONTHLY RENT $
ADDRESS	PHONE

MY SAVINGS ACCOUNT NAME OF BANKS	AMOUNT	CHECKING ACCOUNT BANK

LIST ALL DEBT AND/OR CREDIT REFERENCES - FAILURE TO LIST OUTSTANDING LOANS MAY DISQUALIFY REQUEST.

TO WHOM OWED - ADDRESS	ACCOUNT NO.	DATE INCURRED	ORIG. AMT.	UNPAID BALANCE	PAYMENT AMT.
			$	$	$
			$	$	$
			$	$	$
			$	$	$
AUTO FINANCE			$	$	$

REFERENCE OF PAID UP CREDIT _____ WHEN PAID _____

NAME AND ADDRESS OF	RELATIONSHIP
NEAREST RELATIVE	PHONE

IF JOINT APPLICATION - PLEASE COMPLETE BELOW		
NAME	DATE OF BIRTH	SOCIAL SECURITY NO.
ADDRESS	HOW LONG?	TELEPHONE
EMPLOYER AND POSITION	HOW LONG?	MONTHLY/WEEKLY GROSS INC. $
DEBTS AND/OR REFERENCES		

The statements herein are made for the purpose of obtaining the loan, and are true. I understand that failure to list any outstanding debt may disqualify the request. I/WE hereby authorize the Credit Union or any credit bureau or other investigative agency employed by the Credit Union, to legally investigate any references herein listed or statements or other data obtained from me or from any other person pertaining to my credit and financial responsibility.

DATE _____ SIGNATURE _____

FIGURE 5-5

LIST OF ALL ASSETS (REQUIRED OF ALL BORROWERS)

For purposes of determining your present net worth, you are required to list all major assets you own in part or in full. This is confidential information to help establish your credit worthiness as a borrower.

TYPE OF ASSETS	DO YOU OWN? YES	NO	DESCRIPTION	% YOU OWN	ESTIMATED TOTAL $ VALUE	WHERE LOCATED
REAL ESTATE						
Residence						
Vacation Home(s)						
Investment Property(s)						
Business Property(s)						
Land						
TRANSPORTATION						
Automobile(s)						
Truck(s)						
Van(s)						
Antique Car(s)						
Trailer(s)						
Boat(s)						
Snowmobile(s)						
Motorcycle(s)						
Moped(s)						
Other						
JEWELRY						
Watch(es)						
Ring(s)						
Necklace(s)						
Bracelet(s)						
Pin(s)						
Other						
ANTIQUES/COLLECTIBLES						
Furniture						
OTHER						
Silver						
Bank Account(s)						
Stocks/Bonds						

investigation to determine the applicant's credit worthiness. (No credence should be given to the applicant's answers on the questionnaire until they have been verified by the lender.) The application also should furnish enough additional information about the borrower to assist the lender in locating the borrower or in recovering money owed in the event the borrower becomes a collection account. (For example, references are requested so they may be contacted regarding a lender's whereabouts in the event he or she becomes a "skip" collection account.)

Completing the Application and Conducting the Interview

Every applicant should be required to apply in person and to be interviewed by the loan officer. If an application is accepted by mail—as is the case with many credit cards—the lender must depend on the answers given in the application to be accurate and the lender must further rely on his or her ability to conduct a thorough credit check and to receive complete and correct information about the borrower. Or the lender may rely on a credit-scoring system. However, it is a fact that delinquencies and collection accounts are higher among those creditors who grant credit by mail than on the part of those who grant credit only after a face-to-face interview with the applicant.

Questions asked on a consumer credit application are limited by law to those that do not give the lender an opportunity to discriminate on the basis of sex, race, marital status, or age. Questions are restricted only to those necessary to determine an individual's credit-worthiness and ability to repay. So, the credit application should be designed with care and reviewed by an individual knowledgeable in the law before introducing it. (Figure 5–4 is an example of an acceptable application.)

Once the applicant has completed the application—which she or he should be able to do privately—and brought it to the loan interviewer, the interviewer should greet the applicant with a smile and by name. (The name is known from the application.) If there is more than one applicant (either a joint loan or a cosigner), all applicants should be present at the interview. And, if there is more than one applicant, it is strongly recommended that separate applications be taken from each person who will sign the note of obligation.

Before proceeding to check over the application, the reviewer should establish the identity of the applicant through some positive means of identification. Notes should be made of the identification provided and should be kept with the application in the lender's file. It is not uncommon for a thief intent upon defrauding a lender to apply for credit under a false name, And, even if the applicant is known to the reviewer identification should be required. On occasion, a thief will establish a relationship under a false name with a lender and then capitalize on the familiarity that has been built up with the reviewer to apply for a substantial loan with the intent to defraud the lender.

The interviewer should then review each question on the application verbally, even though it has already been answered in writing. For example, the basic question of "NAME?" can be approached by asking: "The correct spelling of your last name is: S-M-I-T-H?" The interviewer should then print next to the name legible printing. If a question has not been answered and after asking the applicant why it is not, if it is not applicable, that should be noted on the application: "N/A." If there are a number of questions receiving "N/As" for answers, the application should be evaluated with extreme care.

Correctness is a necessity in every credit application, especially in the spelling of names, in addresses, and in phone numbers. The interviewer should make certain to the best of her or his ability that all of these are correct. If an applicant does not know or remember the address or phone number of a former employer or a reference, it should be determined at the time of the interview or before the application is finally accepted and acted upon.

The interviewer should ask any other questions that are not on the questionnaire (and not prohibited by law) that might be pertinent and he or she should take notes during the interview of any facts or observations that might have a bearing on processing the application. For example, if an applicant has had a recent job change and therefore does not have the length of time on the job normally required to be granted credit, a few questions might reveal the existence of an employment contract that guarantees a job and salary for several years.

The loan interviewer should be thoroughly trained in all federal and state laws governing consumer credit. When assisting an applicant with the application, the interviewer must give proper ECOA warnings and must avoid any questions that could be in violation of such laws. The interviewer should also be capable of calculating loan payments and should know how to quote Annual Percentage Rates so all regulations are properly met.

When the application has been completed to the interviewer's satisfaction, the applicant should sign it in the presence of the interviewer so the interviewer can verify that the information on the application was actually provided by the same person who signed the application.

Reasons for the Application Questions

The application questions and the answers provided and subsequently verified serve two purposes. They are the basis either for granting or denying credit, and they aid in collecting the loan if it goes into default. The references given become sources of information if the debtor cannot be located. The List of Assets can be used if the debtor goes to bankruptcy court and pleads insolvency. Answers about debt status which may later prove to be false can be used if legal action is taken against the debtor. (See figure 5–5.)

Processing the Application

Following the applicant's departure, the interviewer should make a few notes about his or her impressions of the applicant and note any suggestions he or she might have to guide the person who must make the determination whether or not to extend credit to the applicant. A "loan number" should be assigned to the application and a customer file folder and file card reflecting this number prepared. The application and all notes made by the interviewer should be placed into the file together with the customer file card.

Customer Information Card File (Index Card or Computer)

Perhaps the most valuable record a credit department can have is a Customer Information File (C.I.F.). While this may be maintained on index cards, it is even more effective if it is computerized. Color-coded cards filed alphabetically by customer name and cross-filed numerically by social security number should be set up for each account the customer establishes, then melded and maintained together so a complete composite picture can be had at any time of a customer's past and current activities. At least two types of index cards should be maintained for loans: collateral and installment. These cards provide the loan officer with immediate information of all open loans, declined loans, paid loans, and collection loans. Until the final disposition of the loan is determined, status information should be entered in pencil. When a customer's credit activity ceases, these cards should be moved from an active to a "paid loan" file where they will continue to be filed alphabetically as loan numbers will no longer be relevant (except for social security number). When there is a credit request, both the opened and closed customer card files should be reviewed to determine whether there is a history of either present or previous contact.

If a loan becomes delinquent, a separate collection card should be prepared and incorporated into the card file record system.

What About Credit Scoring?

Because it can take several years to develop the expertise necessary for a loan officer to be able to judge the credit worthiness of credit applicants, Ben had turned to credit scoring as a way by which his inexperienced people could make rapid credit decisions about the applications they processed. But, this was back in the 1960s before the advent of the Equal Credit Opportunity Act and Regulation B. Also, this was long before credit scoring had developed into a fine art and computers were brought into play to analyze available credit data. Today, credit scoring has become a sophisticated tool used by many of the nation's leading consumer lenders. Judgmental processing of consumer credit applications is rapidly being assisted and in some cases replaced entirely by computerized credit scoring systems. This is becoming even more the case since the ECOA now permits the use of a credit scoring system if it is "demonstrably and statistically sound and empirically derived."

Ben's primitive credit scoring system was a mass-produced product developed by a New York bank and sold to retail lenders all over the country. It did not take into consideration the specific characteristics of a given lender's markets, customers, and past history. On the other hand, today's sophisticated systems are custom designed for every lender. Lenders can spend from $10,000 to $50,000 to develop a system for themselves, with cost dependent on the size of the customer base and the sophistication of the system they select.

A modern credit scoring system is the association of an accumulation of creditor data with good and bad credit risks. Numerical values are assigned to specific demographic characteristics to reflect the amount of risk a lender takes in granting credit. The point scoring is based on a statistical analysis of a scientific sampling (usually about 3000 good and bad loans plus 300 charged-off loans). The sample is then applied to a mathematical model and weights are given to a series of factors found to be most relevant in evaluating an applicant's credit worthiness. A numerical value is then assigned to the several possible answers to a series of questions about the applicant. Credit is then granted or denied based on the total score achieved.

Through the use of a credit scoring system it is possible for lenders to predetermine their volume of business, to control their losses and delinquencies, to be aware of the quality of business they are putting on their books, and to monitor their performances. Business volume is determined by selecting scores for approving or denying loans which either increase or decrease the volume of business written. Losses and delinquencies are controlled by eliminating those applicants whose scores fall into the high risk area. Loan quality can be determined by where the majority of approved applicants fall on the numerical scale. And scoring permits the lender to keep track of the performance of the loans granted by pointing to the scores that lead to losses. (See figure 5–6.)

Before deciding whether or not to incorporate a credit scoring system into the retail lending operation, a lender should consider a number of questions: How will the use of a credit scoring system affect your customers? How will it affect your credit department personnel? What will its effect be on your present loan volume? Are your current loan delinquencies and charge-offs so bad that another measure is needed to reduce them further? What is the cost of instituting a credit scoring system? How will it reduce your present credit costs?

If a decision is made to institute a credit scoring system, the lender should seek out a system designer with the proper expertise and extensive experience. To attempt to self-develop a credit scoring system is to court disaster. Credit scoring is most feasible for large-volume lenders especially when the numbers of applicants reach such a volume that indepth interviews with each credit applicant becomes impractical. (See figure 5–7.)

FIGURE 5–6 Measuring risk with credit scoring. Typical debt repayment probability measure based on typical credit score.

CREDIT SCORE	REPAYMENT PROBABILITY
50 & Under	0%
60	10
70	20
80	30
90	40
100	50
110	60
120	70
130	80
140	90
150 & Over	100

The Credit Check and Verifying Customer Data

After taking the application, the data given by the customer must be verified and the credit worthiness determined. Customer data is verified by telephone calls and letters. Careful records should be kept of all information received from the reference supplied. For example, written notes should be placed in the customer's file indicating: "Telephoned employer—12/1/83. Thomas Jackson of Personnel Department verified employment from 2/76 to present. Salary verified."

All references given should be confirmed. Check customer's home telephone by calling. Verify home address from street directory or telephone book. Call personal references and tell them the applicant gave their name as a personal reference and you are calling to inquire about his or her character. Above all, check all credit

FIGURE 5-7 How credit scoring determines good and poor credit risks. 1. Borrowers' characteristics are analyzed and rated ("Discriminant Analysis"). 2. Scores are assigned to sampling of good loans and loans that have gone bad. 3. Distribution of scores are charted and cut-off score determined as well as a judgmental area where both good and bad loans fall and credit scoring cannot predict results.

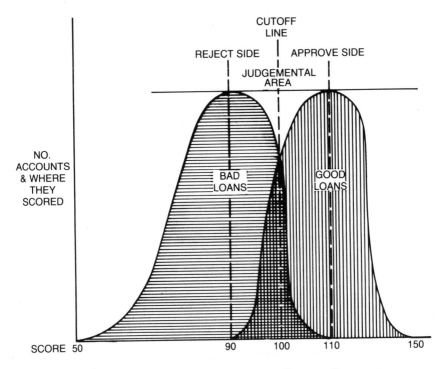

references. Call banks, department stores, other creditors. Contact both local and national credit bureaus for complete credit check on the applicant. Ideally, the lender is a member of the credit bureaus and linked to them by computer so all that is necessary is to type in the borrower's name, address, social security number, and an access code. The computer will then produce a credit file on the applicant.

With all data confirmed and credit worthiness determined, the loan officer can then make an educated decision whether to grant or deny credit or to suggest an alternative offer to the applicant.

Notifying the Applicant of the Credit Decision

Once the loan officer has made the credit decision, the applicant must be notified of that decision regardless of what it is. If the application is approved, a telephone call is adequate to make the decision known. However, it is strongly recommended that notification be made in writing as well and that a copy of the notification letter be kept in the customer's loan file. (A sample letter follows.)

SUBJECT: Your Loan Application Approved.

Dear Customer:

Congratulations! We are pleased to inform you that your application for (a credit card/a loan for $____/a $____ line of credit) has been approved. Please plan to visit our office within the next five days to sign the necessary loan note and to activate your loan. Call the undersigned for an appointment so it will not be necessary for you to wait when you arrive.

Sincerely,

Frequently, loan applicants apply to several sources for a loan and it is the lender who first notifies the applicant of the approval that gets the business. If the applicant fails to come in after having been notified of the approval, a follow-up letter should be sent:

Dear Customer:

A recent review of our records indicates that your application for a loan has been approved and is still pending. To keep our files current, would you please inform us if you will be activating this loan or not. Simply check the appropriate box and return this letter in the enclosed stamped and addressed envelope. Or, telephone the writer if you prefer.

If you decide that you do not wish to activate a loan at this time, we shall be pleased to retain your application in our files for future reference.

Sincerely yours,

___ Yes. I will be in to activate the loan on _____.
(DATE)
___ No. I do not need the loan at this time.

If the loan is denied, Regulation B requires that the applicant be sent a "Decline Notice" in which the creditor states the reason for the denial and the source of the information which resulted in the denial. (See figure 5–8 Denial Form.)

If a counter offer is made to the applicant (lesser amount than requested, shorter or longer terms, etc.), it should be put into writing and sent to the applicant with a copy in the applicant's file. If the counter offer is not accepted, then a "Decline Notice" should be sent. If the counter offer is accepted, the change should be noted on the application and the applicant called in to sign the note.

The Loan Note

Basically, there are two types of loan notes: those for unsecured loans and those for collateral loans. These clearly state how the loan interest is to be calculated by listing the total number of payments, the amount of each payment, the final payment, any finance charges, the amount financed, and the annual percentage rate (A.P.R.) (See figures 5–9, 5–10.)

For simplicity and uniformity, it is recommended that the two types of notes be similar in appearance because the basic system each follows is the same. The only difference is in some of the wording. Size or color coding could be used to differentiate each type of note. Because the note is a legal document and the prime obligatory instrument that binds the debtor to the creditor, there should be no errors in completing it. If a correction is necessary, the debtor must initial the change. However, if a correction is necessary, it is preferable to prepare a new note. A lender never knows what a court of law might decide as to the acceptability of an obligatory note.

As can be seen from the samples, a note must include or reflect the following:

- Total principal dollars due.
- Date of the contract.
- Payee and payor.
- The amount of each payment due.
- The date when the first payment is due and when subsequent payment are due.
- The interest—or interest and principal—that must be paid with each payment.

- Other facts such as the collateral for the loan and any state and federal statutes that are applicable.

- Additional forms for the execution of the collateral being held.

- The recording of such types of collateral as required by law.

- Margin requirements as the law indicates for certain types of real or negotiable instruments.

- Cost factors involved with defaults.

- The note must state the number of days before the late charges can be added and the maximum percentage of the monthly payment that can be collected.

- Any additional forms required by state or federal laws in connection with secured and/or unsecured personal loans including stock-secured loan Regulation U required forms.

- Truth-in-Lending disclosure statement. (See figure 5–11.)

- Sufficient copies of the note and other forms to comply with all regulations and internal requirements.

- The signatures of all parties committed to repaying the loan. (NOTE: Signatures that pledge and hypothecate [to pledge without delivery of title or possession] collateral, pledge only to the given value of the collateral—not to the full amount of the loan balance due. So, such signators should sign the loan note also.)

- The back of the note can also be used to list other information and provisions. If the back is used, a notice must appear on the front of the note to "see reverse side." The reverse may be used to list:

  - Proof for the correct amount of dollars to be advanced on loan renewals.

  - Federal errors and omissions on open-end loans only.

  - Information about other collateral where there is insufficient space on the note face.

  - Any other information desired.

FIGURE 5-8   Denial Form

STATEMENT OF CREDIT DENIAL,
TERMINATION, OR CHANGE

DATE _____

Applicant's Name: _____

Applicant's Address: _____
_____

Description of Account, Transaction,
or Requested Credit: _____
_____

Description of Adverse Action Taken:
_____
_____

PRINCIPAL REASON(S) FOR ADVERSE
ACTION CONCERNING CREDIT

_____ Credit application incomplete	_____ Temporary residence
_____ Insufficient credit references	_____ Unable to verify residence
_____ Unable to verify credit references	_____ No credit file
_____ Temporary or irregular employment	_____ Insufficient credit file
_____ Unable to verify employment	_____ Delinquent credit obligations
_____ Length of employment	_____ Garnishment, attachment, foreclosure,
_____ Insufficient income	repossession, or suit
_____ Excessive obligations	_____ Bankruptcy
_____ Unable to verify income	_____ We do not grant credit to any applicant on
_____ Inadequate collateral	the terms and conditions you request.
_____ Too short a period of residence	_____ Other, specify: _____

DISCLOSURE OF USE OF INFORMATION
OBTAINED FROM AN OUTSIDE SOURCE

_____ Disclosure inapplicable
_____ Information obtained in a report from a
consumer reporting agency

Name: _____

Street address: _____

Telephone number: _____

_____ Information obtained from an outside source other than a consumer reporting agency. Under the Fair Credit Reporting Act, you have the right to make a written request, within 60 days of receipt of this notice, for disclosure of the nature of the adverse information.

Creditor's name: _____

Creditor's address: _____
_____

Creditor's telephone number: _____

FIGURE 5–9   Security Agreement

Form 7-4 Uniform Commercial Code Massachusetts — Truth in Lending   ORIGINAL
(For use where collateral is Consumer Goods and Promissory Note is used. May also be used for Notes secured by Business or Farm Equipment.)
SECURITY AGREEMENT — (Chattel Mortgage)

_____
(Date)

_____
(Name)   (No. and Street)   (City)   (State)
(hereinafter called "Debtor"), for valuable consideration, receipt whereof is hereby acknowledge, hereby grants to

(hereinafter called "Secured Party") a security interest in, and mortgages to Secured Party, the following property and any and all additions and accessions thereto (hereinafter called the "Collateral"):

to secure payment of the Total of Payments as evidenced hereby and by the note or notes of even date herewith and also any and all liabilities of Debtor to Secured Party under this agreement or said note or notes or any renewals or extensions thereof (all hereinafter called the "Obligations"). The Secured Party is the creditor in this transaction.

DISCLOSURES OF THE COST OF YOUR LOAN

Amount Financed—The amount of credit provided to you or on your behalf. . . . . $ _____

FINANCE CHARGE—The dollar amount your credit will cost you . . . . $ _____

Total of Payments—The amount you will have paid when you have made all scheduled payments . . . . $ _____

ANNUAL PERCENTAGE RATE—The cost of your credit as a yearly rate . . . .   _____%

Your payment schedule will be:

Number of Payments	Amount of Payments	When Payments Are Due

Late Charges: If an installment of principal and interest is not received within 15 days after the installment due date, you will be charged 5% of the amount of the payment or $5.00, whichever is less.
Prepayment: If you pay off early, you will not have to pay a penalty, and you may be entitled to a refund of part of the finance charge.
Security Interest: You are giving a security interest in

Filing Fees in connection with the Security Interest: $ _____

Optional Insurance: Credit life insurance and credit disability insurance are not required to obtain credit and will not be provided unless you sign and agree to pay the additional cost.

Type of Coverage		Premium
Coverage Period		
☐ Credit Life		$ _____
☐ Credit Disability		$ _____
☐ Credit Life and Disability		$ _____

I want the insurance options checked above. _____
                                             Signature
You may obtain property insurance from anyone you want that is acceptable to the Secured Party. If you get the insurance through the Secured Party, you will pay the premiums listed below:

Type of Coverage	Coverage Period	Premium
		$ _____
		$ _____
		$ _____

See other portions of your contract documents for any additional information about nonpayment, default, right to accelerate maturity of obligation, and prepayment refunds and penalties. e means an estimate.

The Amount Financed is made up of:

		Amount paid to others on your behalf		Total Amount Financed	$_____
Amount given to you directly	$_____	To public officials	$_____	Prepaid Finance Charge	$_____
Amount paid on your account	$_____	To insurance companies	$_____		
		Prepaid Finance Charge	$_____		

ADDITIONAL PROMISES

You may at any time pay off the full unpaid balance due under this Agreement, and in so doing you may receive a partial rebate of the finance and insurance charges based upon the Rule of 78s if the term of the Obligations does not exceed 54 months, or based upon the actuarial method if the term of the Obligations exceeds 54 months, except that no refund will be made in amounts less than $1, to the extent permitted by law.
In addition to the Late Charge, in the event of default Debtor agrees to pay the reasonable attorneys' fees, to the extent permitted by law.
If the Secured Party is a bank, the banker's right of set-off means that if Debtor is in default, the bank may, without notice, apply funds in the Debtor's checking or other deposit account maintained at the bank to satisfy in full, or reduce, Debtor's debt to the bank.
Debtor hereby warrants and covenants that—
    (a) The Collateral is bought or used primarily for

        ☐ Personal, family or household purposes   ☐ Farming operations use   ☐ Business use

and if checked here ☐, is being acquired with the proceeds of the note or notes, which Secured Party may disburse directly to the seller of the Collateral;

    (b) The Collateral will be kept at _____
                                              (No. and Street)   (City or Town)   (State)
or if left blank, at the address shown at the beginning of this agreement; Debtor will promptly notify Secured Party of any change in the location of the Collateral within said State; and Debtor will not remove the Collateral from said Sate without the written consent of the Secured Party;
    (c) If the Collateral is bought or used primarily for business use, Debtor's place of business in said State (if any) is that shown at the beginning of this agreement; and all other places of business of Debtor in said State outside of the town or city mentioned in the previous clause are located as follows:

    (d) If the Collateral is bought or used primarily for personal, family or household purposes, or for farming operations use, or if Debtor has no place of business in said State, Debtor's residence in said State is that shown at the beginning of this agreement;
    (e) If the Collateral is to be attached to real estate, a description of the real estate is as follows: _____
                                                                                                                                     ;
and the name of the record owner is _____
and if the Collateral is attached to real estate prior to the perfection of the security interest granted hereby, Debtor will on demand of Secured party furnish the latter with a disclaimer or disclaimers, signed by all persons having an interest in the real estate, of any interest in the Collateral which is prior to Secured Party's interest.
If any other agreement between the Secured Party and the Debtor purports to secure the Obligations, the Secured Party expressly waives its rights thereunder with respect to the Obligations. This agreement was executed in the Commonwealth of Massachusetts and shall be governed by the laws of said Commonwealth.
This agreement is subject to the additional provisions set forth on the reverse side hereof, the same being incorporated herein by reference. Debtor acknowledges receipt of a copy of this agreement.
    Signed in duplicate and delivered on the day and year first above written.
(Secured Party need sign only if agreement is to be used as Financing Statement)

_____   _____
(Secured Party)   (Debtor)

By _____   By _____
Form 7-4   Published by Hobbs & Warren, Inc. Boston, Mass. 02101, 1969-1974-1976-1982

FIGURE 5–10   Suggested Proof for Back of All Installment Loan Notes.

STATEMENT OF LOAN

Amount of Loan $_____

Less Discount $_____

Less Fee $_____

Less Balance Previous Loan No._____ $_____

Less $_____

    TOTAL DEDUCTION $_____

Plus Rebate Previous Loan No._____ $_____

Net Proceeds of Note (if received in cash,
                sign below) $_____

Check No._____Bank_____

Because it differs slightly from an unsecured loan note, open-end loan notes are shown in figures 5–12 and 5–13.

Sometimes a charge account agreement is used in lieu of a note when extending credit for the purchase of goods or services. The same laws and regulations that apply to a loan note also apply to a credit agreement. Usually, a retailer of goods or services will combine the credit application with the credit agreement so it is not necessary for the applicant to return in person to execute a separate agreement when the credit application is approved. This approach is especially valuable to those creditors who solicit customers by mail.

The Uniform Commercial Code is frequently invoked by lenders so they can retain a security interest in the merchandise they finance or sell, but the UCC must be used in conjunction with a security agreement in order for it to be effective.

Cosigner's Acknowledgement

If there is a cosigner on the note, be certain that he or she reads, understands, and signs an "Explanation of the Cosigner's Obligations" form before signing the note. (See figure 5–14.) All too often, a cosigner does not understand that by signing a note with the borrower he or she is assuming the same obligation as the borrower to repay the loan. In the event that the primary borrower defaults, the cosigner is required to repay the balance of the loan and he or

FIGURE 5-11   Truth-in-Lending Disclosure Statement.

PROMISSORY NOTE AND DISCLOSURE STATEMENT

Account No. _____

Note No. _____

$ _____ Terms _____ Due Date _____ Date _____

For value received, I, We, the undersigned maker and co-makers, waiving our rights of demand and notice, jointly and severally promise

to pay to the order of _____

_____ (the Creditor) _____
    (Address)

_____dollars

payable in _____ consecutive _____ weekly, monthly payments of $ _____ The first payment to be made on _____

and a like amount every _____ thereafter until the full amount has been paid; the final payment to be $_____.

Any unpaid balance may be paid, at any time, without penalty and any unearned finance charge will be refunded based on the actuarial method if the original term of this loan is more than 54 months; otherwise, any refund will be based on the Rule of 78's; no portion of any Administrative Fee is refundable. In the event of any default in payments as herein agreed the entire remaining balance due on this note shall become due and payable forthwith at the option of the holder hereof. I/We, the undersigned, hereby jointly and severally pledge all paid shares and deposits and payments on shares and deposits which I/we now have or may hereafter have in this credit union, except shares or deposits which may be held pursuant to any "Individual Retirement Trust" or "Keogh Plan" or as an All-Savers Certificate, as security for principal and interest of the loan evidenced by this Note and any refinancing of all or any part thereof, plus interest, default charges, cost or expenses and this credit union may transfer such funds to reduce or extinguish those debts. If the holder of this Note shall place it in the hands of another for collection, we agree to pay a reasonable collection fee.

Default: A Charge of $ _____, shall be due and payable on any installment in default of more than ten (10) days. Maximum default charge on any installment in default is 5% or $5.00, whichever is less.

TRUTH-IN LENDING DISCLOSURE STATEMENT

ANNUAL PERCENTAGE RATE The cost of your credit as a yearly rate.	FINANCE CHARGE The dollar amount the credit will cost you.	Amount Financed The amount of credit provided to you or on your behalf.	Total of Payments The amount you will have paid after you have made all payments as scheduled.
%	$	$	$

Your payment schedule will be:

Number of Payments	Amount of Payments	When Payments Are Due

Security: You are giving a security interest in your _____ account(s).

Late Charge: If a payment is late, you will be charged $ _____ / _____ % of the payment.

Prepayment: If you pay off early, you ☐ may   ☐ will not   have to pay a penalty.
                                        ☐ may   ☐ will not   be entitled to a refund of part of the finance charge.

See your Note for any additional information about non-payment, default, any required repayment in full before the scheduled date, prepayment refunds and penalties, and security interests.

☐ *means an estimate

Itemization of the Amount Financed of $ _____

$ _____ Amount given to you directly
$ _____ Amount paid on your account

Amount paid to others on your behalf:

$ _____ to public officials
$ _____ to _____
$ _____ to _____
$ _____ to _____
$ _____ to _____

$ _____ Prepaid Finance Charge
(N/A means "not applicable")

Insurance: (Applicable *only* if filled in)
Credit life insurance and credit disability insurance are not required to obtain credit, and will not be provided unless you sign and agree to pay the additional cost.

Type	Premium	Signature:
Credit Life		I want credit life insurance. Signature:
Credit Disability		I want credit disability insurance. Signature:
Credit Life and Disability		I want credit life and disability insurance. Signature:

I, the maker, acknowledge that I received a copy of this Note and Disclosure Statement on the above date.

WITNESS   NAME   ADDRESS

_____ MAKER _____   _____

_____ CO-MAKER _____   _____

_____ CO-MAKER _____   _____

FIGURE 5–12   Open End Loan Note

REVOLVING CREDIT   NOTE, PLAN, AGREEMENT AND
TRUTH-IN-LENDING DISCLOSURE

CREDITOR

Account Number

The undersigned member(s) jointly and severally apply for a revolving credit loan plan to be used for provident and productive purposes, and agree with the above named _____ terms below. This document includes a Truth-in-Lending Disclosure and **disclosures required, or additional information permitted, by the Truth-in-Lending Act and Regulations are printed in this type.**

1. Upon approval, the _creditor_ may from time to time make one or more advances to the undersigned member(s) **who may pay the balance in full or in part at any time without penalty except that minimum periodic payments are required on each loan account hereunder regardless of any prepayments, as long as any balance exists hereunder.**

2. The _creditor_ reserves the right to amend or terminate this agreement or refuse any request for an advance at any time for any reason not prohibited by law and such action shall not affect the obligations of the undersigned or any other obligor.

3. For value received and to be received, the undersigned maker(s) jointly and severally (each shall be agent for the other and be responsible for the advances to the other whether with knowledge of same or not) promise to pay _____ all sums advanced from time to time on loan accounts under this revolving credit plan plus a **FINANCE CHARGE (interest) at the periodic rate of**

_____% per day which corresponds to an **ANNUAL PERCENTAGE RATE of** _____%. **The FINANCE CHARGE is computed on any unpaid principal balance(s) for the period such balance(s) is outstanding and is calculated at the time a payment is made; balance(s) change each time new amounts are borrowed or payments are made or credits given.**

4. Minimum payments on each loan account shall be $_____
   ☐ per week
   ☐ biweekly   for each $_____ or fraction thereof
   ☐ semimonthly
   of outstanding principal balance calculated after each advance but not less than

   $_____   ☐ per week.
                  ☐ biweekly.   Minimum periodic payments
                  ☐ semimonthly.
   shall not be reduced even though the principal balance declines as payments are made. Payments shall be due on

   ☐ _____ of each week

   ☐ every second _____ commencing _____
                  (day of week)   (date)
   ☐ the _____ and _____ of each month
   except that: 1) when an advance is made on a loan account having a zero balance, the first payment shall not be due until the second regular due date following the date of the advance, and 2) when subsequent advances result in an increase in the minimum periodic payment, such an increase shall not become effective until the second regular due date following the date of the advance.

5. **Each payment on a loan account will first be applied to retire the FINANCE CHARGE then due and the remainder applied to the unpaid principal balance; any unpaid portion of the FINANCE CHARGE will be paid by subsequent payments and not added to principal.**

6. **(A)** If an amount has been entered on a "Revolving Credit Request Voucher" as "Pledged Shares and/or Deposits," the person signing such voucher hereby pledges such amount of shares and/or deposits, whether held individually, jointly or in trust, as security for any and all moneys advanced under this plan and interest accrued thereon and authorize the _creditor_, in the case of default, to apply same to payment of said obligation.

   (B) Upon default or determination by the _Creditor_ that there has been a substantial adverse effect on the ability to repay of any of the undersigned as a result of a change in status of employment or increase in outstanding obligations, the undersigned hereby pledge all shares and/or deposits and payments and earnings thereon which I/we then or thereafter may have, whether held individually, jointly, or in trust, as security for any and all moneys advanced under this plan and interest accrued thereon and authorize the _creditor_, in the case of default, to apply same to payment of said obligation.

(C) The _creditor_ **shall have the lien on shares and/or deposits for sums due the credit union as provided in the Credit Union Act or other law of this state or the right to impress a lien on shares provided for in the Federal Credit Union Act, as the case may be.**

7. **No security shall be required hereunder if the outstanding balance after an advance does not exceed**

$

In other cases, security consisting of one or a combination of the following will be required:

(1) A co-maker or guarantor,

(2) A pledge of shares and/or deposits,

(3) An assignment of wages,

(4) A security interest under the Uniform Commercial Code or other governing law.

Any interest acquired by the _Creditor_ under **(2) through (4)** above shall:

(A) Secure repayment of all balances outstanding hereunder when the interest is given, and repayment of all subsequent advances hereunder, and

(B) Remain in effect until all such balances have been paid in full; provided, however, that if the total of all outstanding balances hereunder becomes less than the dollar limit mentioned above and there is no default hereunder, the credit union will, upon request, release any or all such security. However, the _Creditor_ will not be required to release statutory or similar liens or rights to liens or shares and/or deposits pledged pursuant to paragraph 6(B) hereof.

8. **No statutory lien nor right to impress a lien and no pledge of shares and/or deposits shall apply to any shares or deposits which may be held pursuant to any individual retirement account or self-employed plan qualifying as such under the Internal Revenue Code.**

9. **Property insurance, if written in connection with any advance under this plan, may be obtained from any person of maker's choice.**

10. **In the event any payment on any loan account hereunder is not made when due, or if an event of default occurs under any security agreement which may be executed in connection herewith, then the entire unpaid balance of all loan accounts under this agreement plus accrued interest shall become immediately due and payable, at the option of the** _creditor_ **upon compliance with applicable law relating to notice. The undersigned further agrees to pay all usual and customary costs of collection permitted by law.**

    In connection herewith, the undersigned jointly and severally waive presentment for payment, demand, protest and notice of protest and dishonor;

11. The failure of the _creditor_ to exercise any of its rights under this agreement shall not be deemed to be a waiver of such right or any other right available hereunder.

12. Undersigned agrees that the _creditor_ is authorized from time to time as it deems necessary to make inquiries pertaining to employment, credit standing and financial responsibility.

13. Undersigned agrees that (a) the _creditor_ may retain this agreement to comply with federal and/or state law and (b) in compliance with applicable law, regulation and this agreement the _creditor_ may change the terms of the plan from time to time upon prior notice mailed to the undersigned's last known address as shown on the records of the _creditor_.

NOTICE: See accompanying statement for important information regarding your rights to dispute billing (statement) errors.

FIGURE 5-12   *(Continued)*

Plan desired: ☐ Individual ☐ Joint with: _____ Relationship _____   Action by, _____

Witness our hand(s) and seal(s) this _____ day of _____, 19 _____

Date ____/____/____
Revolving Credit   ☐ Approved

Account No. _____ (seal)
                         Applicant maker (member) signature   ☐ Rejected

                                                                                                  Paragraph 7 Loan Limit $ _____
Account No. _____ (seal)
                         Applicant maker (member) signature   Conditions, if any, _____

Truth-in-Lending   Copy
Disclosure Received   _____   Mailed _____   _____
                        Member's initials   Date   Staff initials   Date   _____

┌───┐
│ Request for credit card: │   _____
│   In the event, now or in the future, a credit card may be utilized to gain access to the credit │
│   privileges granted herein, I/we request that such a card be issued. │   _____
│   │
│   _____   │   _____
└───┘   Loan Officer

she is subject to the same collection procedures and credit rating as the original borrower. A cosigner is usually required when it is thought that the original borrower may be somewhat weak in his or her ability to repay. Frequently, when the cosigner discovers the extent of his or her obligations in the event of default by the original borrower, the cosigner will then refuse to sign the note.

When the note has been executed, the original copy and all supporting documents (such as a UCC form) should be placed in the customer's loan folder. A folder into which all documentation (except the index cards) can be filed is an integral part of the procedural system. File folders should be filed numerically and cross-referenced to the index file. Collection documents as well as loan documents are to be maintained in the file and, when the loan is finally paid or the credit account closed, the folder should be removed from the active file, marked paid or closed, and refiled in a *closed* file alphabetically because the former loan number is no longer pertinent.

Payment Reminders

Once the note has been executed and the funds dispersed to the borrower—or credit made available to her or him—some form of payment reminder must be created. Usually, the reminder takes the form of a coupon book or a monthly statement or billing. These, of course, may be created either manually or through a computer. Whichever form is used, each coupon or statement must carry on it

FIGURE 5–13   Open End Loan Statement

IN CASE OF ERRORS OR INQUIRIES ABOUT YOUR STATEMENT OF LOAN ACCOUNT

The Federal Truth in Lending Act requires prompt correction of mistakes on your open end loan statement.

1. If you want to preserve your rights under the Act, here's what to do if you think your statement of account is wrong or if you need more information about an item:

   a. Write on the statement of account or other sheet of paper (you may telephone your inquiry but **doing so will not preserve your rights under this law)** the following:

      i.   Your name and account number.

      ii. A description of the error and an explanation (to the extent you can explain) why you believe it is an error.

      If you only need more information, explain the item you are not sure about and, if you wish, ask for evidence of the transaction such as a copy of the credit request voucher. Do not send in your copy of any document unless you have a duplicate copy for your records.

      iii. The dollar amount of the suspected error.

      iv. Any other information (such as your address) which you think will help   to identify you or the reason for your complaint or inquiry.

   b. Send your notice of statement error to the address on your statement of account which is listed after the words: "Send Inquiries To:" or similar wording.

   Mail it as soon as you can, but in any case, early enough to reach   within 60 days after the statement was mailed or otherwise delivered to you.

2.   must acknowledge all letters pointing out possible errors within 30 days of receipt, unless   is able to correct your statement during that 30 days. Within 90 days after receiving your letter, must either correct the error or explain why   believes the statement was correct. Once   has explained the statement,   has no further obligation to you even though you still believe that there is an error, except as provided in paragraph 5 below.

3. After   has been notified, neither   nor an attorney nor a collection agency may send you collection letters or take other collection action with respect to the amount in dispute; but periodic statements may be sent to you, and the disputed amount can be applied against your credit limit. You cannot be threatened with damage to your credit rating or sued for the amount in question, nor can the disputed amount be reported to a credit bureau or to other creditors as delinquent until the credit union has answered your inquiry. **However, you remain obligated to pay the parts of your outstanding balance not in dispute.**

4. If it is determined that   has made a mistake on your statement, you will not have to pay any finance charges on any disputed amount. If it turns out that   has not made an error, you will have to pay finance charges on the amount in dispute, and you will have to make up any missed minimum or required payments on the disputed amount. Unless you have agreed that your statement was correct,   must send you a written notification of what you owe.

5. If   explanation does not satisfy you and you notify   **in writing** within **10** days after you receive its explanation that you still refuse to pay the disputed amount,   may report you to credit bureaus and other creditors and may pursue regular collection procedures. But   must also report that you think you do not owe the money, and   must let you know to whom such reports were made. Once the matter has been settled between you and   must notify those to whom the reported you as delinquent of the subsequent resolution.

6. If   does not follow these rules,   is not allowed to collect the first $50 of the disputed amount and finance charges, even if the statement turns out to be correct.

FIGURE 5–14 Explanation of Cosigner Obligation

READ THIS PAPER THOROUGHLY. DO NOT SIGN IT IF YOU HAVE
ANY QUESTIONS ABOUT WHAT IT MEANS

You are about to become a cosigner of:

_____   a promissory note in the amount of $_____

_____   a single advance under a revolving credit plan
           in the specific amount of $_____

_____   a revolving credit plan under which loans may be
           made to the maker from time to time in any amounts

under date of _____between_____
and the above named creditor.

This is what can happen to you if the person for whom you
cosigned does not pay the debt:

1. You will be legally liable and fully responsible
    for payment of the amounts owed even though you
    are not receiving any part of the loan.

2. You may be asked to pay the amount due even though
    the party for whom you cosigned may be working and
    even though there may be other collateral, and the
    creditor may begin legal action against you to
    collect such amount owing if you refuse payment.

3. If there is more than one cosigner, the creditor can
    sue you alone and is not required to sue any of the
    other cosigners.

4. Nothing shall discharge or satisfy your liability
    except the full performance and payment of the
    legal obligation and indebtedness with accrued interest.

Be sure to read the note or agreement which you will be signing
with the creditor. It contains the terms of your responsibility
to the creditor. This paper does not create your legal liability;
it only explains some of your responsibilities when you act as
a cosigner.

I HAVE READ AND SIGNED THIS PAPER AND HAVE RECEIVED A COPY
THEREOF BEFORE SIGNING THE PROMISSORY NOTE OR AGREEMENT WITH
THE CREDITOR WHICH MAKES ME PRIMARILY AND LEGALLY LIABLE AS
A COSIGNER.

_____   _____
Date   Signature of Cosigner

One copy to cosigner. One copy for creditor.

an indication of the payment due date, any grace period permitted, and any late charges that will be due if payment is not made by the final due date.

Tracking Payments

As part of the total credit system, the lender must create a system for tracking and monitoring payments. To do this most easily and efficiently, a focal date schedule should be established for each type of loan or credit offered. A focal date is simply the day on which loan payments become due. A lender might set up a focal schedule as follows:

Loans alphabetical	*Monthly focal date*
A - F	1 st
G - L	8 th
M - S	15 th
T - Z	22 nd

At the end of the given day, or on the day immediately following, all payment records to date are checked. If the payment has not been received, a reminder notice is immediately generated and sent out to the debtor. The focal date might also be the date on which a statement is generated. If the loan payment has not been made by that date, the past due notice is printed on the statement and late charges are added at the same time.

Seven to ten days after the delinquency, the loan files of all delinquents should again be checked, and if payment still has not been made, the account should be turned over to the collection department. A record of the late payment should also be noted on the index card and the fact that the account has been given to collection.

The Paid-Up Loan

When all payments due have been made and the loan is repaid in full, the "Paid-Up" or "Cancelled" note should be returned to the customer with a covering letter congratulating him or her on a good credit standing, thanking her or him for his or her business, and reminding her or him to look to you for future credit needs.

6

Collecting Delinquent Loans

THE RULES HAVE CHANGED

When Ben went after delinquent college students, collection methods were far more primitive than they are today under the Consumer Credit Protection Act, Title VIII, which was created to eliminate abusive, unfair, and deceptive practices in the collection of debts. Ben's collection problems did not have to do with collecting the debt when he could locate the debtor. His problem was to locate the debtors who lived in other countries.

Today's creditors must follow strict rules and guidelines in their collection practices. While the collection procedures are quite cut and dried consisting of: locating the debtor, contacting the debtor by mail, telephone, or in person, determining what the problem is, arranging repayment, and keeping records, the collection regulations are fraught with admonitions and penalties. (See figure 6–1.)

Before reviewing these restrictions, let's examine the causes of delinquencies and charge-offs and look at some ways delinquencies can be controlled.

The Collection Objective

The collection objective is to obtain payment of money owed and to simultaneously retain the goodwill of the debtor. Not all delinquent customers are bad credit risks. On occasion, late pay-

FIGURE 6–1   Collection Procedures

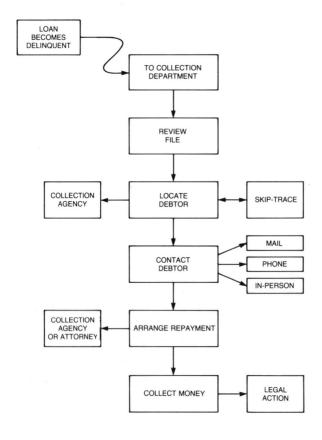

ment will be caused by misunderstanding terms, temporary unemployment or other financial emergencies, or for reasons other than a deliberate effort to avoid paying a debt.

Good collection procedures begin with the acceptance and maintenance of accounts. Therefore, when creditors are in the process of extending credit, they should do so with the thought in mind that this individual could one day become a collection account. So, it is in the creditor's best interest to make certain his or her loan-granting procedures include the following activities.

A Thorough Credit Investigation

The primary means of keeping delinquencies to an absolute minimum is to conduct a thorough credit check on every applicant. If there is a concern that to do a detailed check requires a considerable investment in time and money, the lender only has to charge the credit applicant an application fee to cover such costs or increase the interest charged for the loan so that the return is sufficient to pay for the credit check. Failure to do an adequate credit check on every loan applicant will invariably lead to extreme loss and major collection problems.

A Detailed Explanation of Credit Terms

Credit terms are usually detailed in printed forms which are given to the debtor at the time the loan is granted. All too often the borrower lacks the interest or the desire to read the terms in detail. So, it is the responsibility of the lender—especially if he or she wishes to reduce collections to a minimum—to take the necessary time and effort to explain in detail the credit terms to which the borrower is obligated. The time invested by the lender in reviewing these obligations will pay off for the lender through reduced collections and increased customer goodwill.

A Close Watch on Credit Limits

Once a limit has been set, the customer's account should not be overlooked until it becomes a collection account because the customer exceeded the set limit. This can happen unless the lender routinely examines every credit line. When an account balance approaches the set limit the credit manager can inform the borrower that he or she has only a few dollars left before her or his line is exceeded or the lender can extend the line if the borrower has proved to be one who can handle a larger credit line.

A *Timely Follow-Up on Delinquents*

Experience has proved that debts are easier to collect and collection problems are averted when collection efforts are made as soon as the debt becomes delinquent. It is important that creditors develop a payment-due notice system that reminds the debtors that payments are due together with an early warning system that reaches out to a debtor and demands immediate payment almost the exact instant the loan becomes delinquent.

Collection Procedures

When establishing your collection procedures, you should plan them so they will move in a regular and orderly manner through a series of predetermined steps. The collection effort builds in intensity until a final decisive action is taken. The intent is to bring the delinquent account up-to-date as quickly and efficiently as possible or to get the delinquent loan paid off in full. The collection procedures should be organized into four basic steps:

1. Remind Delinquent Borrowers

Borrowers who do not meet their payment due dates should immediately be reminded that their payments are past due and a request for immediate payment should be made. Also, there should be an assessment of a late payment penalty if payment is not forthcoming.

Manner. The first reminder should be mild in manner because the assumption of the collector should be that the customer has merely overlooked the matter but still has the ability to make the payment. The first effort at collection should be gentle yet firm reminding the debtor that he or she has overlooked the payment due date but that if the past-due payment is made immediately there will be no problem with the account or the customer's credit rating.

Method. The method of the first past-due reminder might take the form of either a phone call or a printed notice. A phone call is the most effective and desirable way to make contact. Because it results in a two-way conversation, the collector can determine quickly if the problem is merely one of oversight or one of far greater danger. For example, by calling a collector is able to determine if a phone has been disconnected. This may be a sign that the debtor is unable or unwilling to pay his or her bills, especially the phone bills, or that the debtor has become a skip. If the phone number has been changed and is now unlisted, the creditor has an indication that the debtor is making an effort to hide from her or his creditors. A phone call at the first sign of delinquency may also determine that a debtor has lost his or her job, is hospitalized, or has some other financial problem. This knowledge will permit the collection department to take preventative action before the account becomes a major collection problem. If the volume of past-dues is too great to permit individual phone calls to each debtor, the collection effort must depend on printed letters or notices mailed to the debtors. If mail is used, it should be either first class or registered mail so the collector can determine if the mail is deliverable to the debtor.

Whether the debtor is reminded of his or her past-due debt by telephone or written notice, the reminder should bring to the debtor's attention the exact amount past-due, the terms of the credit agreement, and a request for immediate payment.

Timeliness. Experience has proved that the longer a creditor waits to pursue a past-due debt, the less successful are the chances of recovery. Therefore, the creditor should establish an early-warning system designed to create a past-due notice almost the instant a payment is not received on the date due. Ideally, the first notice to the debtor should be delivered on the day after the date the payment is due. This is, in essence, what is done with credit card billing. If the payment is not made by the due date, the customer is automatically billed for the added interest even if the payment is received on the following day. Or, as another example, if a depositor writes a check against insufficient funds, the check is bounced on the day it is received even if a deposit is made into the account later in the day. Delinquent loan payers should be notified just as promptly. (See tables 6–1 and 6–2.)

2. Follow-Up When Payment is Not Made

When the initial past-due notice has been made and the debtor fails to respond within seven days from the receipt of the notice, the

TABLE 6–1.   Estimated Loss on Unpaid Loan

How Long Loan Delinquent	% Loss To Expect
90 Days	10%
180 Days	35%
1 Year	50%
2 Years	75%
5 Years	100%

TABLE 6–2.   Loan Value With Age

Age	Value to Lender
Current	100%
2 months past due	90%
6 months past due	67%
1 year past due	45%
2 years past due	23%
3 years past due	15%
5 years past due	01%

creditor can assume that the neglected payment is not just an oversight but that it is caused by some problem the debtor has in coming up with the money owed. Contact should definitely be made by telephone at this stage and an effort made to determine the reason for the payment lapse. Written confirmation of the phone conversation and the agreed-to action should then be made or, if the creditor is unable to reach the debtor by phone, written notice and a demand for immediate payment should be made plus a request that the debtor contact the creditor by phone or in person to discuss the problem.

3. The Collection Effort Underway

If both notices have been ignored, it can be assumed that the debtor does not intend to pay his or her debt at this time, so stronger collection methods must now be employed. These include contacting the debtor by telephone, registered letter, or telegram and notifying him or her that unless payment is made immediately or contact is made with the collection department and some acceptable payment arrangement is made with the creditor, the creditor will take one or a number of actions. These include: suspending credit privileges, notifying the credit bureau of the delinquency, calling in any collateral if there is any, assessing a savings account if there is one and the loan agreement gives that right to the creditor, or turning the matter over to an attorney, to a court, or to a collection agency, or simply intensifying the collection effort.

The Collection Schedule

To be effective, the collection effort should be made according to a predetermined schedule not haphazardly. A typical collection schedule follows:

DAY 1: Payment due

DAY 2: Collection department notified payment not received.

DAY 2: Collection department either sends out past due notice or telephones creditor.

DAY 7: If payment not received, debtor contacted second time by collection department.

DAY 14: Debtor contacted third time if payment still not made. Debtor advised that stronger action will be necessary unless payment is forthcoming or other arrangements are made.

DAY 21: Take threatened action if payment still not received. Notify customer that the action is being taken.

DAY 31: Second payment now due. If a payment is not made at this time, turn account over to attorney or collection agency if not previously done.

Collection Don'ts

DO NOT:

• Threaten to assign the obligation unless you intend to.

• Do not threaten to have the debtor arrested unless you intend to.

• Threaten attachment of wages unless you intend to take judicial action to do so.

• Use profane language.

• Telephone the debtor without disclosing the name of the creditor.

- Make more than two telephone calls a week per debt to the debtor's home and no more than two telephone calls in any 30-day period to a place other than his residence.

- Call at any time other than normal working hours.

- Call the debtor's place of employment (more than 2 times within 30 days) unless the debtor gives you permission.

- Fail to send the debtor a written notice within 30 days following the first communication made to the debtor at his or her place of employment: *NOTICE OF IMPORTANT RIGHTS -* You have the right to make a written or oral request that telephone calls regarding your debt not be made to you at your place of employment. Any such oral request will be valid for only ten (10) days unless you provide written confirmation of the request postmarked or delivered within seven (7) days of such request. You may terminate this request by writing to the creditor.

- Go to the debtor's house other than between the hours of 8 a.m. to 9 p.m. and only make one visit in a 30-day period. You must remain outside the house unless the debtor invites you in.

- Go the the debtor's place of employment unless invited by the debtor.

- Confront the debtor in a public place about his or her debt excluding courthouses, the creditor's place of business, or the office of the creditor's attorney.

- State that you will sue the debtor unless you actually sue within 14 days or you state some other period of time. If an attorney for the debtor informs you that you should only contact the attorney, you must do so.

- Imply the existence of a debt to persons residing in the debtor's household.

- Threaten the debtor that you will tell persons in the debtor's household about the debt.

- Contact persons other than the debtor or any third party and discuss the debt.

Deceptive Collection Practices

Don't make:

1. A false representation to the debtor that you have something of value or that you have information for the debtor, which is of value to him or her.

2. Any representation that an existing obligation of a debtor may be increased by the addition of attorney's fees, investigation fees, service fees, or any other fees or charges, if in fact such fees or charges may not legally be added to the existing obligation.

3. Any solicitation or obtain any written statement or acknowledgement in any form containing an affirmation of any obligation by a debtor who has been adjudicated bankrupt, without clearly and conspiciously disclosing the nature and consequences of such affirmation.

Inspection

It shall constitute an unfair or deceptive act or practice for a creditor to fail to allow a debtor or an attorney for a debtor to inspect and copy the following materials regarding a debt during normal business hours of the creditor and upon notice given to such creditor not less than five business days preceding the scheduled inspection:

1. All papers or copies of papers in the possession of the creditor which bear the signature of the debtor and which concern the debt being collected;

2. A ledger, account card, or similar record in the possession of a creditor which reflects the date and amount of payments, credits, and charges concerning the debt.

It shall be an unfair or deceptive act or practice for a creditor to request or demand from a debtor a postdated check, draft, order for withdrawal or other similar instrument in payment for the debt or any portion thereof, or for a creditor to negotiate such instrument before the due date of the instrument.

4. Charge-Off the Debt and Get Rid of It

When all efforts to collect the delinquent loan have failed, the lender has no option left but to write it off the books as a total loss. However, after charging it off, the lender still has the final recourse of getting rid of the loan by turning it over to a collection agency or attorney. This action is usually done on a contingency basis whereby the agent or attorney extends his or her efforts in return for a percentage (usually 50%) of the monies he or she is able to recover. However, there are some attorneys and collection agencies who work on a fee basis turning over 100% of whatever they collect—but the lender must pay a pre-determined fee with no guarantee of recovering any or all of the delinquent loan.

The Collection Card.

NAME: _____ACCOUNT #:_____

ADDRESS: _____

CITY: _____STATE: _____ZIP: _____

TELEPHONE NOS.: (HOME) _____(BUSINESS)_____

ACTION SCHEDULE AND RESULTS

DATE	ACTION	BY	RESULT	NEXT ACTION	WHEN
	Past Due Rem.				
	Telephone				
	First Letter				
	Telephone				
	Second Letter				
	Telephone				
	Third Letter				
	Refer Outside				

LOAN SUMMARY: Original Amount:$ _____; Del. Bal.: $ _____
Payments (Amount/Date): $_____/$_____/$_____/
$_____/$_____/$_____/$_____/$_____/

Collection Controls

The most effective collection techniques call for a combination of printed notices, telephone calls, and collection letters. Smart collecting suggests that the creditor first develop a procedural system which spells out the action to be taken and the timing for each act. Using this as a guide, the collectors attack each delinquent account referred to them by first setting up a collection card which notes the intended actions and the scheduled dates for the action. Then, using this card as the primary control, the collection department goes into action in a concerted effort to collect the delinquent loan.

Delinquent Follow-Up File

A delinquent follow-up file should be established. This file uses a collection card and is initiated with the advice of a late charge notice on installment loans. It is activated from an overdue report sent to the collection department. At this point, the collection cards for installment loans are filed alphabetically behind a focal date notice marker. All collection work must be recorded on these cards. (Inactive collection cards are stored alphabetically or numerically in a dormant file for future use when the loan is paid to date.)

Each entry on the card starts with a date, describes the action taken, and ends with the date of anticipated payment or action. The physical appearance of this file is as follows:

- *Activator Notice Index Marker*: The collection card is activated on advice on an overdue 10-day late charge notice on installment loans. These are the activators of your collection system. They will then be similar and will meld with ease. Your overdue reports should be generated in conjunction with your *Focal Date Systems* (the dates on which loan payments are due).

- *Letter Index Marker*: Used primarily for accounts that are exceptions and where phone contact with the debtor is not feasible or a memo to senior management is required.

- *Phone Index Marker*: This is the workhorse of your collection process.

- *Alpha Index Marker*: This is the automatic follow-up. No collection cards are to be filed without an "anticipated action," with the date of such action listed last. This truly should be called the "Reminder File."

Each morning the alpha follow-up file is broken down for the anticipated action that did not materialize (the Reminder File). All stale dates are removed and placed back into the work area (phone call or letter acquired).

Each morning, go over the previous day's payments, remove the collection cards that have payments made, and record this fact on the card. If the account is prompt, return the card to the dormant loan file or dormant mortgage file. For those that are still delinquent, a decision must be made as to further follow-up. Put the date on the back as to further follow-up and file it into the alpha follow-up file. The off-set tickets or previous day payment journal may be reviewed the next day, so the collection file is kept current.

COLLECTION LETTERS

Letters are the most frequently used collection tool. Most collectors know that a well-written letter sent to a debtor at the right time can be the most effective and least costly means of communication between borrower and lender. But, there are no standard letters that can be used for the optimum results. The best collection letters are those that are custom-made to appeal to a lender's specific market and circumstances. Such letters fall into four different categories: reminder letters, appeal letters, follow-up letters, and final demand letters. An example of each of these is offered on the pages following. It should be noted that the old saying is still true: "One catches more flies with honey than with vinegar." So, collection letters should always start softly and gently and gradually build up to the toughest talk. Even though the primary purpose of the collection effort is to collect the debt owed, the collector's desire should be to retain the borrower's goodwill and continued business if at all possible.

FIGURE 6–2 Reminder Letter

Dear _____:

This letter is just a friendly reminder that your monthly payment has not yet been received. Your account shows $_____ due as of _____ 19 ____. If you have not already mailed us your payment for this amount, please do so today.

Cordially,

Borrowers who miss a payment and then ignore the first reminder notice have almost always done so intentionally. So, now instead of the "honey" approach, the collector must take a tougher line and use a series of follow-up letters designed to prod the reluctant customer into paying. Typical appeal, follow-up, and final demand letters follow.

FIGURE 6–3 Appeal Letter

Date:_____

Borrower:_____

Loan No._____

Past Due Amount: $_____

Dear Customer:

IS SOMETHING WRONG?

You should be acting now to preserve your good credit standing, but you have done nothing yet to protect it.

A few days ago we sent you a notice that your loan payment was past due for the amount shown above. Despite this notice, you still have not brought your loan up to date. Consequently, we have <u>frozen those funds you have in your savings</u> to be withdrawn and applied against your past-due payment if you fail to contact us at once and act immediately to reinstate your good credit standing with us.

IF YOU FAIL TO MAKE YOUR PAST-DUE PAYMENT WITHIN
ONE WEEK OF THE DATE OF THIS LETTER, WE WILL HAVE
TO TAKE ACTION TO PROTECT THOSE FUNDS WHICH YOU
HAVE BORROWED AND AGREED LEGALLY TO REPAY ACCORDING
TO OUR TERMS.

We can be most understanding if there is a good reason why you have not made your payment up until now. Simply phone the signer of this letter and explain the circumstances. We will make every possible effort to accommodate you if you are encountering financial difficulties as long as you cooperate with us.

But, if you fail either to bring your account up to date or to contact us and make some new accommodations, <u>we will have to take funds out of your savings, turn the matter over to our collection department, and inform the various credit-reporting bureaus of your delinquent status</u>.

Anxiously yours,

_____

Loan Department

FIGURE 6-4 Follow-up Letter

COLLECTION DEPARTMENT

DATE:_____   BORROWER:_____

LOAN #:_____   PAST DUE AMOUNT:$_____

TO THE ABOVE NAMED DEBTOR:

Your loan account has become seriously delinquent and the
Loan Department has turned it over to us for collection.

Previously, you had been sent a "Late Payment Notice"
followed by a letter from our loan department requesting
payment. Both of these moderate appeals have remained
unanswered by you.

Because you have been unresponsive to those efforts to
bring your account up-to-date and to preserve your good
credit standing with us, we have taken funds from your savings
and applied them against your loan. Further, we have notified
various consumer credit reporting agencies of your present
delinquent status. Finally, we now intend to expend every
legal recourse available to us in an effort to collect from
you the entire amount due on your loan, plus whatever late
charges and legal fees may be incurred in so doing. This is
being done under the terms of the Promissory Note you signed
and accepted when you initiated this loan. The terms read:
    "IN THE CASE OF ANY DEFAULT IN PAYMENTS AS HEREIN AGREED,
    THE ENTIRE REMAINING BALANCE DUE ON THIS NOTE SHALL
    BECOME DUE AND PAYABLE FORTHWITH AT THE OPTION OF
    THE HOLDER HEREOF. WE HEREBY PLEDGE ALL OF OUR SAVINGS
    DEPOSITS WHICH WE HAVE IN_____, PLUS INTEREST
    DEFAULT CHARGES, COSTS, OR EXPENSES AND WE AUTHORIZE THE
    HOLDER TO APPLY ALL SUCH DEPOSITS TO THE PAYMENT OF
    SAID LOANS."

However, I wish to advise you that it is not too late to
rectify this very grave situation. You can still make
restitution and begin to restore your credit rating by
coming in, by telephoning us, or by using the enclosed reply
card to make corrective arrangements. But you must respond
immediately on receipt of this letter. If we do not hear
from you and some corrective action is not taken immediately,
we will have to take action against you.

Sincerely yours,

COLLECTION DEPARTMENT

cc: Your cosigner:_____
    YOU ARE NOW OBLIGATED TO PAY THIS LOAN! IF THE
    BORROWER DOES NOT RESPOND, WE WILL SEEK PAYMENT
    FROM YOU!

FIGURE 6–5 Follow-up Letter

DATE:_____

NAME:_____

LOAN NO.:_____

ATTENTION DEBTOR:

Your loan is now more than ____ months delinquent for a past due amount of $_____ and a total amount due of $_____. We have attempted to contact you a number of times by both mail and telephone to inform you of the consequences of this situation. Apparently, you have chosen to ignore our notices and have not responded to our many efforts to help you.

THIS IS YOUR FINAL NOTICE FROM US!

You have a deadline of _____ by which to pay your account in full or to contact us and make some positive arrangement to make restitution. We have been more than lenient in this situation and there will be no more evasions tolerated.

If you choose not to respond to this letter by the above date, the following courses of action may be taken against you:

1. If you own residential property we will instruct our attorneys to place an attachment on your home.

2. If you own any other tangible property of value, we will seek an attachment against that.

3. Your account will be turned over to a professional collection agency.

4. Demand for payment will be made of any cosigners you might have.

5. Both national and local consumer credit bureaus will be notified of your delinquency which may have an adverse effect on your credit standing with both present and future creditors.

6. In addition to the loan balance, you now will be liable for any and all attorney and collection fees incurred.

This letter and information is being extended to you as one last courtesy. Please reciprocate and avoid unnecessary litigation by contacting us immediately.

COLLECTION DEPARTMENT

FIGURE 6–6   Final Demand Letter

```
ATTENTION:
SUBJECT:    PENDING LEGAL ACTION AGAINST YOU!

Few people borrow money from us with the deliberate
intent to defraud.  It has been my experience that
most borrow from us honestly and that they consider
their loans a legal and just personal obligation they
fully intend to repay.

In your specific case, for some unknown reason (perhaps
temporary unemployment or an unexpected illness), your
loan - on which there is an outstanding balance due of
$_____, plus late charges - has not been paid since
_____.

     Your loan has not only become seriously delinquent,
     but you have compounded the seriousness of the
     situation by ignoring all our efforts to help
     you reinstate a proper repayment schedule and
     your original good credit rating.

Before we conclude absolutely that it is your intent not
to repay your legal debt, and before we are forced by your
actions in this matter to seek any possible legal recourse
at our disposal (including the attachment of any real or
personal property you may own), we are offering you one final
chance to remedy this situation.

     YOU HAVE UNTIL _____ AT _____P.M.
     TO RESPOND TO THIS LETTER BY COMING IN PERSON AND
     REPAYING IN FULL OR IN PART AND ESTABLISHING WITH
     US AN ACCEPTABLE REPAYMENT SCHEDULE FOR ANY BALANCE.
     YOUR FAILURE TO CONTACT ME ON OR BEFORE THAT TIME
     AND DATE WILL FORCE ME TO REMAND YOUR CASE TO OTHER
     AUTHORITIES FOR SUPERIOR ACTION.

Manager or Vice President
COLLECTION DEPARTMENT
```

Attributes of Successful Collection Letters

The most successful collection letters are those that are polite, firm, and concise. Such letters should reflect the institution they represent in both content and appearance. In their style and form they should reflect the character of the collection problem and an understanding of the customer. Some of the attributes of an effective collection letter are these:

- It includes the debtor's name and address and is dated. The amount of the past due payment and a description of the merchandise purchased or service rendered (if any) should be given.

- It should be kept as personal as possible. If not individually typed, it should be designed to appear so, with a personal salutation and an individual signature.

- The appeal should be to the debtor's reputation, sense of fair play, self-interest, or his or her fear of future problems.

- There should be a sense of urgency.

- Each letter should be different and should be signed by a different and continually higher authority.

- Wherever possible, delivery should be insured by using certified mail, return receipt requested. An address correction request should be printed on the envelope.

- And, of course, all letters should endeavor to produce a response from the debtor.

Telephone Collection

Although more time consuming than sending out collection letters, telephone contact directly with the debtor can be even more effective than the collection letter which does not produce a two-way dialogue. While a debtor can ignore a letter, it is not as easy to ignore a voice on the telephone. The first telephone contact also gives the caller the opportunity to determine the problem.

The individual doing telephone collection work should be aware of the complete record of the delinquent debtor. The collector should also be thoroughly versed in the collection laws and regulations and in the lender's policies regarding delinquent accounts. The collector should be extremely persuasive, responsive, and a good listener. His or her approach should be businesslike and never abusive or threatening. The collector should recognize that the whole purpose of the telephone call is to recover a debt owed while managing to keep the borrower's goodwill toward the lender.

For both legal and business reasons, the telephone collector must keep a physical record of every phone call made whether or not completed, and of the results of the call. By doing so, the records will assist any future collector who might take over or any lender who might want more information on a borrower.

Other Collection Activities

In addition to the three basic collection activities of telephoning, mailing letters, and calling on the debtor in person, there are several other collection activities that can be employed by collectors. Depending on the type and size of the debt and the willingness of the debtor to cooperate, these range from the physical repossession of collateral to the courtroom confrontation. The range of activities that might be used to aid in debt collection is limited only by federal and state regulations and the ingenuity of the collector.

Repossession

When a loan is secured by collateral and the debtor is either unable or unwilling to repay the loan, the creditor can reclaim the collateral. The act of repossessing (whether surrendering insurance for its cash value or driving off an automobile parked on a public way) is governed by a number of state statutes that dictate how such an action can be handled. Every collector should be familiar with particular laws governing such action in the state in which recovery takes place and should act accordingly. The following text is the actual wording of one state's statutes covering the creditor's right to take possession after a loan is placed in default. This is given only to indicate the extent to which the creditor's right to repossess collateral can be regulated.

Chapter 255, Section 131, General Laws.

(a) In any consumer credit transaction involving a loan that is secured by a non-possessory security interest in consumer goods, a provision relating to default is enforceable only to the extent that the default is material and consists of the debtor's failure to make one or more payments as required by the agreement, or the occurrence of an event which substantially impairs the value of the collateral.

(b) After a default under a consumer credit transaction by a debtor the secured creditor may not bring an action against the debtor or proceed against the collateral until he or she gives the debtor the notice required by this section. Said notice shall be deemed to be delivered when delivered to the debtor or when mailed to the debtor at the debtor's address last known to the creditor. If a debtor cures a default after receiving such notice and again defaults, the creditor shall give another notice before bringing action or proceeding against the collateral with respect to the subsequent default, but no notice is required in connection with a subsequent default if, within the period commencing on the date of the consumer credit transaction subject to this section and the date of the subsequent default, the debtor has cured a default after notice three (3) or more times.

(c) The notice shall be in writing and shall be given to the debtor ten (10) days or more after the default. The notice shall conspicuously state the rights of the debtor upon default in substantially the following form:

The heading shall read: "Rights of Defaulting Debtor under State Law." The body of the notice shall read: "You may cure your default in (describe transaction in a manner enabling debtor to identify it) by paying to (name and address of creditor) (amount due) before (date which is at least twenty-one (21) days after notice is mailed). If you pay this amount within the time allowed, you are no longer in default and may continue with the transaction as though no default had occurred. If you do not cure your default by the date stated above, the said creditor may sue you to obtain a judgment for the amount of the debt or may take possession of the collateral.

If the said creditor takes possession of the collateral, you may get it back by paying the full amount of your debt plus any reasonable expenses incurred by the said creditor if you make the required payment within twenty (20) days after he or she takes possession."

(d) No Court shall enter a deficiency judgment against a debtor which includes a finance charge or insurance premiums allocable to installments due after repossession. A debtor whose goods have been repossesed shall not be liable in a civil action for a deficiency unless the secured party files an affidavit signed either by the purchaser at the sale or by the secured party stating the price for which the goods were sold and the date and place of sale. Such affidavit shall be filed with the complaint.

(e) Unless the secured creditor has first notified the debtor that he or she has elected to accelerate the unpaid balance of the obligation because of default, brought action against the debtor, or proceeded against the collateral, the debtor may cure a default consisting of a failure to pay money by tendering the amount of all unpaid sums due at the time of tender, without acceleration, plus any unpaid delinquency or deferral charges. Cure shall restore the debtor to his or her rights under the agreement as though the defaults cured have not occurred, subject to the provisions of subsection (b).

Section 13J

1. Taking Possession of Collateral.

(a) Subject to the provisions of this section a secured creditor under a consumer credit transaction may take possession of collateral. In taking possession the secured creditor under a consumer credit transaction may proceed without a prior hearing only if the default is material and consists of the debtor's failure to make one or more payments as required by the agreement or the occurrence of an event which substantially impairs the value of the collateral, and only if possession can be obtained without use of force, without a breach of peace and, unless the debtor consents to an entry, at the time of such entry, without entry upon property owned by, or rented to the debtor.

(b) Except as provided in subsection (a), a creditor under a consumer credit transaction may proceed against collateral only after a prior hearing. In any proceeding where possession of the collateral is part of the relief sought by a creditor, no Court shall allow a secured creditor to take possession of collateral until the right of the creditor to take possession has been determined at a hearing at which the debtor has an opportunity to be heard, having been notified in writing of such hearing at least seven (7) days in advance thereof.

(c) The debtor under a secured consumer credit transaction may redeem the collateral from the creditor at any time within twenty (20) days of the creditor's taking possession of the collateral, or thereafter until the creditor has either disposed of the collateral, entered into a contract for its disposition, or gained the right to retain the collateral.

(d) The creditor may after gaining possession sell or otherwise dispose of the collateral. Unless displaced by the provisions of this section and section 13I, the rights and obligations of the parties, including redemption and disposition of the collateral shall be governed by the provisions of Part 5 of Article 9 of the Uniform Commercial Code. If, in connection with a consumer credit transaction which involves an unpaid balance of $2,000.00 or less and which is at the time of default secured by a non-possessory security interest in consumer goods, the creditor takes possession of or accepts surrender of the collateral, the debtor shall not be liable for any deficiency. If the agreement between the creditor and debtor provides that the debtor is to obtain insurance protecting the collateral against fire, theft, collision or other hazards and naming the creditor as loss payee and if, prior to the repossession or surrender of the collateral, loss or damage occurs which would give rise to insurance proceeds under the terms of the policy in force, then nothing in this section shall be deemed to limit the creditor's rights to so much of the insurance proceeds as does not exceed the fair market value of the collateral existing just prior to the loss or damage and, if insurance as required by the agreement is not in force at the time of the loss or damage, nothing in this section shall be deemed to limit the creditor's rights in proceeding against any third party who is responsible for the loss or damage in the name of the debtor or otherwise. For the purposes of this section the unpaid balance of a consumer credit transaction shall be that amount which the debtor would have been required to pay upon prepayment.

(e) If the unpaid balance of the consumer credit transaction at the time of default was $2,000.00 or more, the creditor shall be entitled to recover from the debtor the deficiency, if any, resulting from deducting the fair market value of the collateral from the unpaid balance due and shall also be entitled to any reasonable repossession and storage costs, provided he or she has complied with all provisions of this section.

(f) Any secured creditor obtaining possession of a motor vehicle under the provisions of this section shall, within one (1) hour after obtaining such possession, notify the police department of the city or town in which such possession occurred, giving such police department a description of the vehicle involved.

(g) In a proceeding for a deficiency the fair market value of the collateral shall be a question for the Court to determine. Periodically published trade estimates of the retail value of goods shall, to the extent they are recognized in the particular trade or business, be presumed to be the fair market value of the collateral.

(2) *Disposition of Collateral.*

The disposition of collateral in consumer transactions is essentially the same as that for commercial transactions. The principal difference is that if the debtor has paid 60% of the cash price in the case of a purchase money security interest in the collateral or 60% of the loan in other cases, the secured party must dispose of the collateral under §9-504 unless after default the consumer has waived the right in writing. Failure to so dispose of the collateral within ninety (90) days after repossession entitles the debtor to sue the creditor for conversion (i.e., the fair market value of the collateral) or for at least 10% of the debt or time price differential plus 10% of the cash price.

Debtor Accommodations

The aim of the collection effort should be to collect a debt without the necessity of taking legal action or involving a third party (e.g., an attorney or collection agency). The lender should make every effort to sit down with the debtor, determine his or her exact circumstances, and work out a repayment plan that will return all or a substantial amount of the debt owed to the lender. Sometimes it might be necessary and wise to compromise and reach an agreement with a debtor to settle for less than the total amount of the outstanding debt. Such an agreement might be worked out in those cases where the debtor has the immediate ability to repay only a portion of the debt and a more remote ability to repay the entire debt even over an extended period of time. Because of the "time-value" of money, and the cost, time involved, and unpredictability of legal action, a debtor accommodation by working out a reduced payment might be advisable.

Accelerated Payment

In those cases where the debtor once again has the ability to repay a loan which has been in default, the creditor should make an effort to establish an accelerated payment schedule so that the remaining debt is paid back in larger amounts and in a shorter time period than originally scheduled.

Wage Garnishment

It is still possible to attach the wages of an employed debtor who disregards his or her obligation to repay a debt. Under present consumer protection regulations however, it is necessary for the creditor to determine and prove a debtor's employment and income and then to seek a judgment from a court of law which will permit wages to be garnished. Many consumers are of the opinion that, under today's consumer protection regulations, their wages cannot be touched nor their employers notified of their debt. This is not the case. So, in a difficult collection case, one recourse might be to point out to the debtor that the creditor has the legal right to seek a wage garnishment action. However, if the creditor threatens wage garnishment he or she must be prepared to take immediate action to do so.

Small Claims Court

One remedy the collector can look to when all reasonable efforts to collect a bad loan have failed is to seek relief through Small Claims Court. Such an action permits the creditor to file for a small fee and to do so without legal counsel if desired. A courtroom hearing usually takes place within a short time of filing and a decision is made by a judge or referee on the spot. Because rules and procedures for small claims action vary from state to state, collectors should familiarize themselves with the local laws governing such action and then determine whether or not Small Claims Court action should be sought with regard to specific debts.

Criminal Court Action

If fraud can be proved in conjunction with the loan application or in subsequent actions by the debtor in connection with the loan itself or with its repayment, the creditor can seek relief from the debt by seeking criminal court action. This course usually does involve attorneys, the compiling of evidence, and the consumption of time and money. But, if the amount involved is substantial and the collector has the desire and the resources, and the guilt of the debtor is obvious, a criminal court action can result in recovery of the debt plus all of the costs involved. This is achieved through the judge's ruling when a guilty verdict is reached. In such cases, the judgment will usually call for the full repayment of the debt and all costs involved in bringing the action.

1099-MISC

When a delinquent loan has been written off totally as uncollectible, there is one last action a collector can take before turning the loan over to a collection agency or an attorney. Obtain from the U.S. Internal Revenue Service a 1099 Miscellaneous Income form. Complete the form and send the recipient copy to the debtor together with a letter informing him or her that unless the loan is repaid in full within 10 days (or makes arrangements with you to repay it) you will send the enclosed form to the IRS and to any state or local tax agency reporting that the debtor has received the amount charged off from you. Because the borrowed funds have not been repaid they now represent income to the debtor which he or she should have reported to the tax authorities and on which he or she now should owe back taxes and any penalties for failing to report this income. The fear that the U.S. Government will grab the debtor for nonpayment of taxes will occasionally bring about immediate repayment of a debt all but written off. If the debtor fails to respond, be sure to send the report to all the concerned tax agencies. Note: This course of action—using a 1099-MISC form when all else has failed—can only be followed if it is the standard practice in all collection cases. It cannot be applied discriminately!

7

Credit Counseling

A PERSONAL BUSINESS

Counseling people who have credit problems is a very personal and confidential business but, it can be a very good business for the smart lender because it can prevent loan loss and increase loan business. Every borrower is different. Each has his or her own special problems, not the least of which is the need to turn to a knowledgeable and sympathetic expert for advise when he or she has credit problems. Credit counseling is usually needed when people have gotten into substantial debt and find themselves unable to cope with the demands of their creditors.

A growing number of financial institutions have recognized the value of offering a credit counseling service. Not only is such counseling the source of additional fee income if the institution chooses, but it can reduce or eliminate collection activity, prevent bankruptcy loss, and develop new and profitable lending business. Those financial institutions that have developed such a service have found it to be a profitable addition even when it is made available free of charge to its customers.

Part of the Collection Program

The lender that has a collection department as a part of its total credit operation is ideally suited to offer a credit counseling service to its customers. The borrower whose account has reached the collection department is an excellent candidate for credit counseling and the smart creditor should consider the possibility of extending an offer of credit counseling as an early step in the collection process. (This is covered in more detail in chapter 5.)

Exploring the Problem

When a troubled debtor finally admits that he or she has a problem and is willing to turn to a credit counselor for help, there are a number of things that should be explored (in confidence, of course) by the counselor. These include:

1. Total debt commitment
2. One-time debts (e.g., secured personal loan)
3. Reoccuring debts (e.g., monthly mortgage payments)
4. Annual income from all sources
5. Possibility of additional employment
6. Deferred payment possibilities
7. Realistic monthly payment schedule
8. Possible reduction in expenses (e.g., cut out cigarettes)
9. Plan for deferring or extending payments
10. Possibility of consolidating debts
11. Communicating with creditors
12. Total commitment by debtor to solve the problem

Resolving the Problem

There is no problem that does not have some solution. Every debtor willing to put herself or himself into the hands of a credit counselor should be assured that there is a solution to the problem of overwhelming debt, providing the debtor is willing to make a total commitment to resolving the problem and to follow the recommendations of the credit counselor completely. In general, the available solutions to every credit problems are these:

1. Cease all future uses of credit until such time as the immediate problems are resolved.
2. Arrange with creditors to rewrite some or all outstanding loans to make payments manageable.
3. Lender to grant a debt consolidation loan which pays off all other debts and creates one manageable payment.
4. Obtain additional sources of income adequate to accommodate the existing debt burden.
5. Seek an accommodation or settlement with all creditors.
6. Failing all else, seek relief through bankruptcy.

Cease Use of Credit

The very first thing the credit counselor must do if he or she is to help a debt-burdened customer is to obtain a total commitment of his or her sincerity from the debtor and from any other person involved with his or her debts. Like giving up cigarettes or liquor, the troubled debtor must agree to give up debt. This is usually accomplished when the counselor requires the debtor to bring in every single one of his or her credit cards and to destroy them in the presence of the counselor. The debtor and any other person involved with the debts should then sign an agreement that he or she will not commit himself to any additional credit without the approval of the counselor or until the present debt problem is resolved. Although such an agreement is not legally binding, the formality of signing it can have a favorable effect on the debtor and act as a deterrent to future temptations.

TYPICAL AGREEMENT

I/We the undersigned, acknowledge an excessive and overwhelming burden of debts totalling $_____$. It is my/our intention and firm commitment to overcome this problem by agreeing to cease all borrowing and credit purchases unless reviewed with and approved in advance by the undersigned credit counselor.

Accepted by: _____

DEBTOR(S)

Witnessed by: _____ Date: _____

CREDIT COUNSELOR

The Family Budget

The wise credit counselor will insist that the debtor immediately establish a family budget, one by which the debtor consolidates all sources of income and allocates every penny towards paying for the basic necessities: food, rent, clothing, medical care, taxes, and debts. The credit counselor should help the debtor set up a realistic budget by which he or she can live and abide until the delinquency problems are overcome. A debtor in severe financial trouble should keep track of every penny of income received and spend it only according to a carefully planned—and strictly adhered to—budget.

Debt Consolidation Loan

If, after thoroughly investigating the debtor's situation, the creditor is convinced that the debtor has the ability and desire to repay all debts providing the monthly total payments can be reduced and extended, the creditor can offer a debt-consolidation loan. Such a loan might repay some or all outstanding debts: it will substantially reduce the monthly payments required so that they can be more easily met. Usually, the lender issues checks payable to both the debtor and the creditors who are to be paid off by the debt-consolidation loan.

Rewrite Loans

The easiest and most effective way of reducing debt is to reduce the size of the monthly payments so that they become manageable within the debtor's available budget. This can be best accomplished by contacting all creditors and explaining the debtor's financial problems and offering to rewrite the outstanding loan balance in a way that will reduce and extend the monthly payments.

Additional Sources of Income

A debtor should be counseled to seek out other sources of income to supplement the primary income source which has proved inadequate to repay the current outstanding debts. Additional income may be obtained from several possible directions. The most obvious is to find a second job, full or part-time, no matter how menial it may seem. The objective is not to find job satisfaction but to eliminate problem debt. Temporary employment could provide the extra income needed to meet the debt obligations. Another income source is to suggest that the debtor liquidate some of his or her valuable possessions and use the income from them to pay off his or her debts. One of the most obvious is to sell an expensive automobile. If needed for transportation to and from work, an inexpensive used car can be acquired. Another income source is life insurance. Frequently, insurance policies have accumulated cash value which could be used to defray debt. A debtor also might be able to generate additional income by selling a certain skill or service he or she possesses such as refinishing furniture, repairing cars, cooking gourmet meals, or typing letters and documents. Every possible source for generating additional income should be explored by the debtor and credit counselor. One of these ways might prove the way to eliminate the debt burden.

Settle with Creditors

One of the most effective services the credit counselor provides is to arrange a settlement with all the creditors. This is usually done on a third-party basis whereby the credit counselor sends a notice to all creditors outlining the debtor's problem, the desire to repay, and a suggested repayment schedule which is within the debtor's financial ability. If the majority of the creditors accept the suggested repayment plan, the monthly debt burden is reduced to a workable amount. The debtor then sets aside a weekly or monthly sum sufficient to make the revised payments and sends out the individual checks to the creditors. (See figure 7–1.)

As previously noted, this type of credit counseling can prove an additional profitable service for a financial institution. It offers several benefits: 1. A way of taking a loan out of the collection department and getting repaid; 2. Prevention of loan loss and charge off; 3. Rescue of a good future customer; 4. Deposit of additional funds into

FIGURE 7-1 Repayment Plan Letter

2 Parts
1-Lender
2-Credit Counselors

TO: (CREDITOR)
FROM: XYZ BANK CREDIT COUNSELING DEPARTMENT
SUBJECT: DEBT CONSOLIDATION TO AVOID THE BANKRUPTCY OF:
(Debtor's Name and address)
_____

    The above-named currently owes you $_____ according to the information provided to us, and has outstanding debts totaling $_____*. He/She/They (have, has) an annual income of only $_____ which comes from (employment/welfare/etc.).

(list source)

Rather than seeking relief from this excessive burden through the Bankruptcy Court, he/she/they (is, are) offering the following extended payment plan which, if acceptable to you and the other creditors, will assure that the total debt is repaid in full and that our client's good credit rating is maintained.

    XYZ BANK CREDIT COUNSELING DEPARTMENT
has been authorized by_____

(Name)
_____

(Address)

to send you $_____ per month for the next ____ months beginning on ____19____ and ending on ____19____.
This will repay in full the outstanding debt including all interest charges and fees if the payment schedule is met as outlined.**

    ACCEPTED BY: _____

(Name, Title)

    FOR CREDITOR: _____

(Name)

    DATE:_____

If acceptable, please return original no later than_____so payments can begin on the date scheduled. (DATE)

IMPORTANT: If you cannot accept this proposed repayment plan, please notify us immediately so we can advise our client of any further possible action open to him including Chapter 7 Bankruptcy.

Sincerely,

XYZ BANK CREDIT
COUNSELING SERVICE

__ We refuse to accept the terms and conditions stated above.
REASON: _____
COUNTER PROPOSAL: _____
BY: _____FOR: _____

(Creditor)

* List of obligations attached.
** Client willing to sign new loan contract to rewrite debt according to schedule offered. Send loan papers if desired.

the financial institution (as weekly payments are made, they accumulate in a savings account until funds are released to other creditors); 5. If desired, the financial institution can charge a fee for providing this service, usually a percentage of the monthly debt payment.

Relief Through Bankruptcy

Bankruptcy should be suggested only as a last resort solution to the debt problem. Unfortunately, a few attorneys today are building businesses by recommending bankruptcy when other solutions to financial problems frequently can be found. However, most other solutions do not produce much income for attorneys whereas bankruptcy proceedings are quite profitable to the attorneys who specialize in it. The credit counselor, especially one who is protecting his or her own loan to the debtor, should avoid suggesting bankruptcy altogether. But, if there is no other alternative, the credit counselor should suggest that the debtor see a reputable bankruptcy attorney. If possible, the counselor should suggest that the debtor select a Chapter 13 filing rather than a Chapter 7 because the Chapter 13 offers some repayment possibility whereas the Chapter 7 virtually frees the debtor from every obligation he or she has and offers almost no payback possibility.

8

Helping the New Borrower Establish Credit

CULTIVATE CUSTOMERS

Borrowers are the lenders' good customers and are to be encouraged and cultivated. When the first-time borrower comes to you, you should do everything in your power to make a customer of her or him. But, what if there is no established credit history?

The Tyro

She has just turned 18, graduated from high school, and has taken her first full-time job as a waitress at a local restaurant. She comes into your loan department and informs the loan officer that she wants to borrow $1,000 to buy a used car so she can commute to work. She has no credit history and no savings to use as security for the loan. Your established lending policies do not permit the loan officer to give her a loan under the circumstances as presented. Distressed because the loan officer has told her she will undoubtedly be ineligible for the loan, she asks: "How does a new borrower establish credit?"

The Loan Officer's Advice

The loan officer tells her, "In the American economic system, it is important that you establish credit as soon as you can. Ours is a capitalistic society where all men and women can benefit monetarily from their abilities to work, to earn, and to borrow money. When you establish a good credit rating for yourself, you can borrow money which you can use to further your education or to buy a house, a car, clothes, or luxuries you would not otherwise be able to afford. Credit is your key to better things and is the means by which Americans improve their lots in life. The problem is how does one go about establishing credit for the first time? Let me suggest a plan of action for you.

"The first thing I want you to do is to visit several large department stores and ask for their credit applications. Chances are good that one or two of the stores will approve your application to make a specific purchase of a small amount because you do have a job and their loan requirements are not usually as strict as ours. Of course, as I suggested, they may limit you in the beginning to a relatively small amount that you can purchase on credit but that doesn't matter. What does matter is that if they do approve your credit application, you are well on your way to establishing a credit history. Over the next few months, make several purchases on credit at those stores. These can be for very small amounts—$5 or $10—but be absolutely certain to repay these loans promptly and in accordance with the terms and conditions of each store.

"Next, apply for several gasoline credit cards. You can get applications at most gas stations. Again, it's much like the department stores, it's probable that one or two of the oil companies will issue you a credit card, especially when you are able to list a department store as a credit reference. If you do receive a card from one or more of the oil companies, use it to purchase small quantities of gas, oil, or auto repairs, and be sure to repay promptly and according to the company terms and conditions.

"Now, visit any of the local merchants with whom you or your family may have done business while you were in high school such as the local drug store, clothing store, or even the pizza parlor. Explain to the owner or manager that you are trying to establish credit so you can eventually borrow money from the bank to buy a car. Ask if the manager would be willing to sell to you on credit for the next few weeks the merchandise which you have always bought for cash in the past. Tell the manager that you would only intend to do this for a month or so—just enough so you can list that business as one with which you have established credit when you apply for your car loan or other credit. If you are known to the manager as an old and good customer, chances are good that he or she will be willing to go along with your request.

"Finally, find yourself a cosigner—a person with established credit who would be willing to cosign your $1,000 loan application. This could be your mother or father, some other relative, or a close friend. Explain to whomever you ask that you have not yet established credit and that you need $1,000 to buy a car to commute to work. Ask your relative or friend to cosign a loan application for you and you will be only too willing to sign an agreement with them to repay the loan to them if, for some unknown or unanticipated reason, you failed to repay the bank and they had to. Also offer to put their name on the automobile ownership papers as further security if they wish.

"If you are able to get a cosigner or if you have established credit with department stores, oil companies, and local merchants, return here to the bank and reapply for your loan. If, at that time, you still have your full-time job and either a cosigner or the established credit references, chances are good that I will give you the $1,000 loan. By the time you have repaid the loan (if you pay it on time and according to our bank's terms and conditions), I can assure you that you will have established credit which will permit you to borrow in future years from other lenders."

Another Approach

In addition to the approach suggested by the loan officer, an individual who wants to establish credit for the first time at a financial institution may be able to do so by building up a savings account and borrowing against it. While this may sound like a secured loan (which most lenders will not recognize for purposes of establishing credit), some lender may be willing to set up an unsecured loan for a saver. The borrower and the lender both agree to freeze savings exactly equal to the amount of the loan (including interest) with the understanding that should the loan go into default, the balance due can be taken out of the savings. As the loan is repaid, the amount of frozen savings is reduced accordingly. The loan itself is written as an unsecured loan and the borrower's repayment history is reported to the credit bureau or to other lenders requesting credit information.

Of course, there are other possible ways of establishing credit if one is willing to seek them out and to make a major purchase or two. There are a number of sellers of "big ticket items" who are willing to sell on credit because the items they sell are not usually delivered in full until the obligation is paid in full. Or, the seller retains a security interest in the merchandise which secures it sufficiently so that if the loan is not repaid, the merchandise can be recovered. The best known example is insurance. An insurance salesman is only too happy to write a policy calling for monthly payment of premiums. If the premiums are not repaid, the policy is simply cancelled and the insurance company has lost nothing by extending credit. The same holds true when one joins a book club or purchases a set of encyclopedias on time. As long as the purchaser makes his or her monthly payment, the books continue to be sent. Fail to pay and the books stop coming. Almost anyone, regardless of his or her present credit standing can make such installment purchases. And, by doing this can begin to establish a credit history. A person who desires to build up his or her credit can also subscribe to magazines or join a record club or make mail order purchases by noting on the mailed-in coupon or application: "Bill me." The seller never seems to question the buyer's ability to pay and is always willing to fill the initial mail order. Failure to pay according to the terms and conditions of the seller will result in the cancellation of the contract and a negative credit report. Whereas, if payments are made promptly and properly, the buyer continues to establish a good credit rating with that particular seller which can be used when applying for credit elsewhere.

Credit Unions

Credit unions came into being for the express purpose of making credit available to those individuals unable to obtain credit from any other source. Generally speaking, it is far easier for an individual with little or no credit history, to borrow from a credit union and, in so doing, to establish a credit rating. Most individuals have the opportunity to join a credit union. There are more than 20,000 of them all over the United States associated with companies, churches, organizations, and communities. Membership usually requires only some association with the credit union sponsor (work for the company, be a member of the church or organization, live in the community) and a $5 deposit into a share savings account. Once a person is a member, he or she can usually obtain a loan according to the policies and practices of the credit union. Typically, a credit union will grant a loan to a member not to exceed a set amount providing he or she has been a member for a certain period of time and agrees to repay through an automatic deduction from his or her regular paycheck. Many such loans are granted whether or not a credit union member has established credit elsewhere. Credit union membership is an easy path to establishing a good credit rating and can be a sound recommendation for a lender to make to the potential borrower who asks: "How do I go about establishing credit?"

9

Analyzing Loan Costs and Pricing Loans

GONE ARE THE GOOD OLD DAYS

Many bankers would like to see a return to the good old days of lending when interest rates were more or less constant and the spread between interest paid on savings deposits and interest earned on loans was a constant and dependable source of profitability. Unfortunately, the good old days of a stable economy appear to be gone forever. Today, financial institutions lend money in an entirely different and constantly changing environment. For a lending institution to operate successfully in this day and age it must know its costs of making a loan and then price its loans so that they return a profit to the institution.

Determining Loan Costs

What does it actually cost you to make a loan? A number of studies have been made over the years, and an average cost of between $25 and $35 for a simple consumer loan seems to be typical. However, each lender who sincerely desires to price his or her services for profitability should do his or her own analysis and determine the actual costs for each type of loan offered.

The Cost Accounting Way

Cost accounting for financial institutions is not an exact science, unfortunately, because of the mixture of indirect and intangible services plus the direct and tangible ones provided. Because of the many different operational methods and techniques used throughout the financial industry, the figures that apply to one type of institution will not apply to another. Clearly, each lender must do his or her own analysis of loan costs if he or she wishes to create a reasonable profit margin and to set competitive prices for his or her various loans. To do an accurate cost study, a financial institution must be prepared to invest a number of days and a certain amount of manpower into doing the job. Those institutions that have done such costing studies in the past (and there are very few that have) indicate that it is a major undertaking marked by a need to pay close attention to those details that are available while sometimes finding it necessary to make arbitrary decisions. It is strongly recommended that an institution that wants to determine its actual loan costs hire an outside agency to do the job rather than trusting the job to its own employees. Insiders are not usually objective. And, they may not possess the skills and knowledge required to do an accurate determination of the costs involved in making and maintaining a consumer loan.

The Factors Involved

To determine the loan costs for a given institution, it is necessary to examine, measure, and price four distinct groupings: space, supplies, service, and labor. It is recommended that these be analyzed on an incremental costing basis rather than measured on a direct or full absorption basis. This is suggested because the incremental costing approach measures only those costs actually associated with the loans whereas direct cost analysis includes other things such as the work performed by employees not directly associated with the lending functions. (For example, direct costing would measure a bank teller's time in accepting a loan payment, even though the bank would have to employ the teller regardless of whether or not he or she had to accept loan payments.) And, full absorption costing is an even more complex process as one must determine all direct costs, all incremental costs, plus an allocation of costs of occupancy, support services, and general overhead.

Space

The first incremental cost that should be determined is the space allocated exclusively to carrying out both the lending and collecting functions. Most institutions assign a specific area for lending because of the private nature of borrowing. However, some smaller institutions do not have separate areas for lending and may use a platform officer's desk as the loan desk in which case there may be no incremental space cost to calculate. However, in those cases where specific space has been designated solely for carrying out the lending and collecting functions, the annual cost of renting, leasing, or owning that space must be determined. Also, a determination must be made of the cost of all the furniture, fixtures, and equipment required solely for use in the lending and collecting areas and the annual depreciation cost must be taken into account.

Supplies

All of the loan forms used, the stationery needed for corresponding with the borrowers, the statements mailed out to them, and the coupon books or passbooks used to record the loan payments are simple costs to determine. Also to be included are the costs of postage, collection forms and letters, record cards and file folders, and any computer forms or paper that must be purchased. Don't overlook other supplies such as pens, pencils, paper clips, and scotch tape.

Services

There are a number of services connected with the consumer lending function. And each of these should be costed and factored into the cost of making a loan. Services to be measured incrementally are: telephone costs (including the collectors' phone costs), utilities (electricity and heat), computer services, insurance costs (especially if free life insurance is given with the loan), advertising costs (only those ads promoting loans), collection costs, and special service costs (such as credit checking and street directories).

Manpower

To determine the cost of manpower, measure only the individuals involved who have been hired specifically to use a majority of their time performing lending and collecting functions. Do not measure the time of a bookkeeper or a teller, for example, even though they may spend some portion of their time performing some work related to lending or collecting. To determine the costs of various lendings functions, specific things to measure are the average times involved in taking a loan application (how much time a loan officer spends with each applicant reviewing the application); judging the application (how much time it takes to review the application, check the references, run the credit check, reach a decision); processing the loan (how much time it takes to send out the approval or the rejection, how much time it takes to make out the note and any other forms that might be involved such as insurance applications, how much time it takes to cut and issue the check for the borrowed amount, how much time it takes to put the loan on the computer or into the repayment system and to order the coupon book or make up the passbook or other vehicle used to record the payments); maintaining the loan (how much time is required to monitor the repayments or to send out late notices); collecting the loan (how much time a collector spends on collecting the average defaulted loan); and closing the loan (how much time is required to pay off the loan and cancel and return the paid-up note and to issue a rebate if one is due). For the most part, however, manpower costs need not be broken down unless the lending personnel are concerned with several types of loans, in which case the time spent processing each type must be determined.

TYPICAL LOAN COST ANALYSIS

SPACE

1000 sq. feet @ $10/sq. ft. annually $10 × 1000		$10,000
Depreciation on furniture, fixtures, and equipment ($25,000 depreciated over 5 years)		5,000
		$15,000

SUPPLIES

Loan applications (1 year's supply)	12,000 @ .03¢	360
Insurance applications "	9,000 @ .05¢	450
Denial forms "	4,000 @ .05¢	200
Acceptance forms "	8,000 @ .05¢	400
Notes "	8,000 @ .05¢	400
Coupon books "	8,000 @ $2.50	20,000
Statements "	8,000 @ .025¢	200
(Mailed annually to show interest paid)		
Late notices (1 year's supply)	7,800 @ .02¢	156
Collection letters "	4,000 @ .02¢	800
Mailing envelopes "	50,000 @ .015¢	750
Postage "	50,000 @ .20¢	10,000
File folders "	15,000 @ .05¢	750
Record cards "	15,000 @ .01¢	150
Computer forms "	24,000 @ .03¢	720
Miscellaneous supplies "		400
		$35,736

SERVICES

Telephone costs (1 year)	$ 6,000
Utilities-electricity and oil (1 year)	3,600

Computer services	"	12,000
Insurance	"	40,000
Advertising	"	24,000
Miscellaneous	"	12,000
		$97,600

MANPOWER

3 Loan officers (Annual salaries and benefits)		$60,000
2 Collectors	"	40,000
2 Clerical	"	25,000
		$125,000

	Annual Total Loan Costs	$273,336
	÷ Total number of applications ÷	12,000
	Average cost per application = $	22.78

What to Do About It

Once a financial institution has determined its actual cost of processing a loan (and some may be shocked when they determine the actual cost of taking in a loan application) there comes the question of what the institution should do about it. Many institutions have simply charged an application fee sufficient to cover the costs involved. Others have factored the cost into the interest rate they charge on the loan. The majority of institutions have overlooked the existence of such a cost over the years and merely assumed that the return they received from the interest they charged for the loan was more than adequate to cover the costs of taking in and processing the loan. If the costs are not to be covered by charging a fee, it is imperative that the financial institution factor it into the loan costs they charge. One of the most obvious things that must be done is to set an absolute minimum amount that will be loaned out by the institution and the time period of the loan. It is obvious that in the example given, the financial institution would not even cover the basic cost (never mind make a profit) if it were to give out a $300 loan for 6 months at a 20% annual percentage rate. This institution would be well advised to set a $500 minimum for a minimum one year term even for a secured loan.

Establishing the Rate

The pricing of loans (what interest rate to charge) is an art unto itself. All too often, a financial institution determines the rate it will charge for the various loans it offers based on what the competition is charging. This is obvious from the way banks react to the changes in the prime rate. When it changes up or down they change. Yet, it may be that the rate which will produce a profit for one bank will not product a profit for another. Rate should be based on a bank's costs and the spread it requires to cover all costs and to make a profit for the institution. In years past, many banks sought a spread of between 300 and 400 basis points. And, because of usury ceilings or federal or state regulations they have been unable to make a profit on the loans they have given out in the past. It would appear that in today's runaway economy, restrictions on interest rate charges are becoming a thing of the past. Today, a financial institution has the legal ability to charge interest rates high enough to assure a profit and they are receiving legal rights to offer new and different types of loans. These loans can have escalator clauses structured into them to permit rate changes that will reflect the changes in the value of money. This will enable financial institutions to realize a fair return on money loaned out for an extended time period. The eighth decade of the Twentieth Century has seen the demise of a number of financial institutions through merger or acquisition by a larger or healthier institution. The major underlying cause behind this trend has been that the cost of funds paid out by the institutions has been rising more rapidly than the yield on assets, especially loans. A series of concepts are suggested that may be used by a financial institution in developing a loan pricing strategy.

The examples used are representative of financial institutions in general. They do not fit any particular institution but can be applied to savings and loan associations, mutual savings banks, credit unions, commercial banks, or to any non-depository institution involved in consumer lending. The examples are based on the following assumptions: 1. the balance sheet of the lender consists only of regular savings and consumer loans; 2. the lending institution pays 5½% interest and charges 15% interest on loans. It must be recognized that these are hypothetical rates and do not reflect a lender's true-effective-rate-to-loan-yield because of varying cash flows, interest computation methods, delinquency rates, etc. For purposes of illustration, assume that the rates given are the effective rates. Further, assume that the lending institution has made a study of operating expenses and reserve requirements, and has determined that their need is 600 basis points. The following spread analysis shows that the lending institution has a gross spread of 950 basis points, a net spread of 450 basis points, and an operating margin of 200 basis points.

SPREAD ANALYSIS
Loan Yield - 1500 basis points
- Cost of Funds - *550 basis points*
Gross Spread - 950 basis points
- Operating Expenses - *450 basis points*
Net Spread - 500 basis points
- Reserves - *300 basis points*
Profit Margin - 200 basis points

It now becomes necessary to consider average revenue (total revenue divided by quantity), marginal cost (the change in total cost which results when an additional unit is added), and marginal revenue (the change in total revenue associated with the sale of an additional unit). So, in the spread analysis shown, the average cost of funds is 5½% (5.5/100) and the average revenue from loans is 15% (15/100). Every new dollar in additional savings the lending institution takes in results in an increase of interest paid out of 5½% (5.5%) and each new loan dollar granted generates revenue of 15¢ (15%). At this optimum situation, the lending institution has a situation where the average cost equals the marginal cost and the average revenue equals the marginal revenue. Each new dollar in savings adds to the institution's costs the same amount as the dollars already there. Each new dollar loaned out adds as much to the institution's revenues as do the loans already outstanding. In this optimum environment, the need for pricing loans for profitability doesn't really exist. And this was the case for financial institutions from the 1930s through the 1970s.

Then the liability mix changed dramatically for America's financial institutions. With the elimination of Regulation Q and the introduction of money market certificates and money market fund accounts, interest rates paid on savings today far exceed the rates savers once received from their savings in America's financial institutions. The spread between the cost of funds and the yield on loans has been substantially reduced. The result is that money added to the basic savings in an institution will result in a marginal cost of the new savings dollar which is far greater than the average cost of basic savings. Thus, the average cost of funds has been rising. It is a mathematical fact that when marginal cost is greater than average cost, then the average cost will be rising. When the marginal cost is less than the average cost, then the average cost will be falling. And when the marginal cost is equal to the average cost, then the average cost will be at a minimum.

When pricing loans, it is necessary to determine how the available funds are going to be used (which will be available for loans and which will be available for investments); and the necessary spread that must be earned on loans in order to meet the desired level of net operating margin. To do this, it is necessary for the financial institution to have a cash flow forecast available plus an estimate of the cost of funds anticipated. Then, the institution should develop a spread analysis which will enable them to determine how much is required to cover operating expenses, reserve requirements, and desired earnings. Finally, they should have an analysis of the competitive marketplace to determine where borrowers are finding the most desirable rates.

One major goal of any forecasting technique is to reduce any error which is bound to creep into the process and to create a means whereby any deviation can be discovered in a relatively short period of time and then to trigger corrective action.

A basic function of any financial institution is to "borrow short and lend long." That is, they must be capable of absorbing a mismatch risk. Since the maturity of liabilities (deposits) tends to be shorter than the life of assets (loans) in a volatile interest rate environment such as the one that exists in the 1980s, a significant change in an institution's net operating margin can develop in a very short period of time.

A loan pricing strategy must be developed to cope with this problem. Pricing strategies are suggested for both traditional fix rate loans whether secured or unsecured and for the new type of variable or adjustable rate loan.

A strategy for loan pricing must include an estimate of the cost of funds available, a measurement of the necessary spread, a determination of who is to bear the risk, and a decision on how to structure the loan contract.

Cost of Funds

The primary thing that must be done is to determine as best as can be done, the cost of funds that will be lent. An effort should be made to determine the average cost of funds over the life of the loan. To compensate for potential error in the interest rate forecast and the projection of the ever-changing liability interest rate as funds are deposited into changing money market certificates or money market funds, an adjustment factor must be included in any pricing decision. This can be done by raising the loan rate above what it looks like it needs to be, by accumulating capital to absorb the risk, and by charging higher loan rates over time. Currently, the conventional fixed-rate loan places the entire mismatch risk on the lender and none on the borrower.

The variable rate loan is designed to pass all or a substantial portion of the risk on to the borrower. This type of loan has been designed to reduce the errors associated with estimating the cost of funds in the future. Since it's not possible to track the cost of funds on a daily basis and to adjust loan rates every time there is a small change in the cost of funds, all errors cannot be eliminated, they can be merely reduced. This reduction is achieved by developing an index designed to approximate the cost of funds. This index may be the Treasury Bill rate, the Prime Rate, or any other well-recognized indicator of the cost of money in the U.S. economy.

Whether making a conventional loan or a variable rate loan it is necessary to compute the financial institution's spread requirements. That is, one must know the amount that must be earned over and above the cost of funds to achieve a desired level of operating margin.

In the case of the open-end loan (particularly as used with credit cards), the fixed interest rate approach has already been somewhat modified. And for any loan, the way that the payment is determined is to multiply the loan balance (a declining balance) by the interest rate and divide the total payments by the maturity of the contract in order to get the equal payment schedule. (Dollar Balance × Rate ÷

Maturity = Level Payment.) This level payment is usually determined from a rate table which includes all of the relevant variables that are fixed over the life of the contract.

With the open-end loan, the maturity is considered a "shifting constant maturity" since the loan could be paid off or extended at almost any time. In the case of the open-end loan, if the borrower receives no further loan advances after the initial borrowing, the maturity remains constant and the payment is level until the loan is repaid. If, however, there are other loan advances, the dollar maturity is then adjusted to a new minimum level payment. In other words, the payment is predicated on the outstanding balance.

A variable rate loan may be set up as one with a variable maturity date, a variable payment amount, or a renegotiable rate with a fixed maturity and a fixed payment —with a balloon payment due at the time of maturity adjusted for the changes in rates which may have occurred during the life of the loan. Of these three types, a financial institution might choose to offer one with a variable maturity. When a change in the index triggers a change in the interest rate, this in turn triggers a change in the total remaining loan balance. A loan based on the variable maturity and the fixed payment is adjusted by the payment remaining level. However, the remaining maturity is adjusted to compensate for the change in the remaining loan balance brought about by the change in interest rate. The alternative to this is a variable payment, fixed maturity loan. In this, when the loan rate changes, the payment due is adjusted to include the rate change but the maturity date of the loan remains the same.

The renegotiable loan begins with a fixed rate for a relatively short period (usually one to five years). Payment are amortized for some longer period. At the date of the loan maturity, if there is any remaining balance due to the renegotiating of the original rate, that amount is due as a balloon payment or may be refinanced at the rate the institution is then offering.

Risk Sharing

As noted earlier, the conventional consumer loan places on the lender the entire risk of a mismatch of interest rate charged to the cost of funds available. A variable rate consumer loan can pass all or a portion of the risk to the borrower. Obviously, the consumer has a built-in bias against a variable rate loan in which he or she has no control over future payments and no idea what they will be in the future or if he or she will have the wherewithal to meet the payments. Variable rate mortgages have been in use by financial institutions since the mid-1970s and variable rate loans based on the prime rate have been offered to businesses by commercial banks for a number of years. In the case of the variable rate mortgage, these were usually written so that they had a maximum amount by which the rate could change in both the short run and over the life of the mortgage. It's possible that an institution that is considering offering a variable rate consumer loan might also wish to place a cap on the loan rate and, perhaps, even a floor in the event of a future downturn in rates. In the case of the variable rate loan, the rate should be slightly below the rate of fixed rate consumer loans because the borrower is sharing the risk and the financial institution has a greatly reduced risk of losing anything on their investments. This, of course, would not hold true if it suddenly became obvious that the index was going to decline in the near future and would stay down over the life of the loan. In such a case, the financial institution should set its variable rate interest higher than the fixed interest loan rate or not offer the variable rate loan at all.

LOAN PRICING STRATEGIES IN SUMMARY

A loan pricing strategy must be based on a full understanding of the lender's current and expected future position. The pricing decision for consumer loans can be based on a careful analysis or can be done in a haphazard manner. Ultimately, the borrower must pay for the pricing decision consequences. If loans are priced incorrectly in the borrower's favor, the lender assumes the risks and needs to have a higher level of capital reserves to absorb the risk than if the interest rates charged were based on more realistic and accurate predictions about the future cost of funds. In the past, some of the risk involved in lending at "lost leader rates" could be passed on to the savers in the form of lower interest rates paid on savings. However, savers today are more sophisticated than in previous years and they are no longer content to subsidize borrowers but want the maximum interest the institution will pay for the use of their funds. The borrower will have to pay for this either through the payment of higher fixed loan rates or variable rate consumer loans. Competition for consumer savings in a world without Regulation Q will virtually dictate the introduction of variable rate consumer loans if institutions expect to compete for savings deposits.

In that soon-to-come time when Regulation Q is a thing of the past, there will be no interest rate ceilings and no maturity limits on savings. Each institution will be forced to look to its own needs for funds and its ability to use the funds it receives to make money for the institution. That will be reflected in how it prices the loans it sells.

CONSUMER LOAN COST ANALYSIS

	TYPE OF LOAN	
	INSTALLMENT	COLLATERAL
	%	%
1. Interest rate % (Gross yield)	_____	_____
2. Cost of money*	( )	( )
3. Cost of insurance**	( )	( )
4. Reserve for losses***	( )	( )

5. Cost of operations (% of total institutional costs):

Salaries and fringe benefits of lending and collecting personnel	_____	_____
Processing costs		
Furniture	_____	_____
Stationery and forms	_____	_____
Accounting and computer service	_____	_____
Total cost of operation	( )	( )

NET YIELD _____ ⌐   _____ ⌐

* Cost of Money= Financial Institution: Current average interest rate paid for deposits received.

Retailer: Current interest rate funds lent would have earned if invested.

** Cost of Insurance= Premium paid by lender for any free insurance coverage given with loan.

*** Reserve for Losses= Base on percent of previous year's loan losses. If no history, use 1%.

⌐ NET YIELD: Usually a minimum of 5% spread over actual cost of loan required to produce profit for lender (depending on the lender's business needs).

10

Bankruptcy and Consumer Lending

THE GROWING ESCAPE FROM DEBT

Most borrowers are honest and have every intention of repaying their loans. The alert lender sometimes can identify the
dishonest borrower when he or she originally applies for a loan. A
proper evaluation of his or her application can disclose dishonest
tendencies, thus giving the lender adequate warning and reasons for
denying the loan application. Any applicant who distorts or gives
obviously false facts should be denied a loan otherwise the lender
may find himself or herself with a bankrupt borrower a few months
down the line. The borrower who is planning to file for bankruptcy
will, on occasion, attempt to feather his or her own nest as much as
possible by applying for loans under false pretenses just prior to the

actual filing. Frequently, if he or she possesses a credit card or has charge accounts, the applicant for bankruptcy will continue to charge right up to the day he or she files. Such deceit can usually be uncovered by the alert lender and appropriate measures can be taken to protect against loss.

The Problem Is the Honest Borrower

The problem arises with honest borrowers who develop financial problems after their loans have been granted and then seek relief through the bankruptcy courts. Today, prudent lenders who practice proper loan application review and analysis techniques as outlines in this book will find that the majority of their loan losses will be due to the unexpected bankruptcy of the honest borrower. Before the liberalization of the United States Bankruptcy Laws, consumer bankruptcy was relatively rare. But, with the "carte blanche" expansion of the Bankruptcy Code in 1979, there has been an explosion in the number of consumers seeking debt relief by taking advantage of the permissiveness and ease with which debt can be forgiven under the new rules. Further, the stigma of bankruptcy is no longer a concern to many borrowers who have decided to follow the road to bankruptcy in order to avoid repaying their just and legal debts—even in those cases where the debtors had the wherewithal to repay if they desired. The revised Bankruptcy Code has become the easy way out for the honest borrower, who in the past would have eventually repaid. Also, because of the revised Code, some attorneys and debt counsellors now make it a practice to recommend bankruptcy to their clients because of the ease with which relief can be obtained.

Identifying the Potential Bankrupt

The wise lender will make every effort to smoke out and exclude the potential bankrupt at the time the application to borrow is made. It is then that the lender has the opportunity to take the various steps necessary to pinpoint those borrowers who may eventually declare bankruptcy. The most obvious and important procedure is to include in the loan application questions about past or potential bankruptcies. Ask your applicants such questions as: "Have you ever filed for bankruptcy? Do you now have an application for bankruptcy pending? Do you plan to file for bankruptcy during the next twelve months?" If they answer positively, you can and obviously should deny their applications. If they answer in the negative and then do file for bankruptcy, you may have legal grounds on which you can stand before the Bankruptcy Court and argue against permitting the borrowers to go into bankruptcy because of established intention to defraud by giving false information on their loan applications

In addition to asking questions about past or planned bankruptcy, the prudent lender can determine the loan applicants' possessions and investments of value which must be declared when a request for bankruptcy is filed. By requiring all credit applicants to file such an inventory with their application, the lender has an indication of their net worth. Then, if bankruptcy is filed in the future, such a listing can be compared to that filed with the court. If a debtor has failed to list all of his or her possessions that were itemized at the time of applying for his or her loan, the lender again has legal evidence to bring before the court for use in arguing against granting the request for bankruptcy. Such an argument might be that the applicant failed to list all of his or her assets when he or she filed for bankruptcy—or, the applicant may have fraudulently stated the value and/or possession of certain assets at the time he or she applied for the loan—or, the applicant may not have listed as assets property that was recently purchased on credit which would have increased his or her debt obligations and given the lender grounds for denying the loan.

A Few Examples

Just about every institution that extends credit or lends money has been taken in by some debtor who has made use of one of the following ploys:

1. The borrower has bankruptcy in mind when she comes to your financial institution and applies for a loan. Because bankruptcy has not yet been filed, a credit review does not show anything adverse. The debtor goes on a borrowing and credit-buying binge until credit is denied and collection action is taken. At that point, the debtor files for debt relief through bankruptcy.

2. At the time the borrower applies for a loan or credit, he or she does not have bankruptcy in mind but he or she does have an extensive debt portfolio. However, the borrower appeals to the lender's good nature, promises priority repayment, offers a cosigner, or otherwise creates the strong impression that your debt has every chance of being repaid. Shortly after getting the loan, the borrower files for bankruptcy.

3. This borrower has a good track record with your institution. He has had several loans over the past years. The borrower says nothing to you about his intentions. Instead, he applies for the maximum amount of money you can or will lend him. Based on his past history you give it to him. He failed to tell you that he was on the verge of losing his job, getting a divorce, or being sued. After getting the loan, he immediately files for a Chapter 7 or Chapter 13 bankruptcy.

Chapter 7 Bankruptcy

Chapter 7 of the Bankruptcy Code provides for the total liquidation of one's personal debts incurred before filing for bankruptcy, except any taxes that might be owed. Through the liquidation of all but certain exempt assets, the debtor is totally freed by the court of all debts on record without having any further obligation for future repayment. Chapter 7 of the Code differs from Chapter 13 in that, under Chapter 13, the court permits the debtor to extend his or her obligations and repay all or part of them in proportion to his or her ability to repay from future income.

How Chapter 7 is Invoked

When a debtor makes use of Chapter 7, he or she files his or her petition in bankruptcy in a Federal Court. At the time of filing the debtor is required to pay a filing fee. He or she is also required to file a list of all his or her obligations together with the names and addresses of the creditors, a list of all his or her assets, and a statement of his or her financial affairs. Once the debtor has filed, the law now refers to him or her as a "debtor" rather than as a "bankrupt" and an "Order for Relief" is given to him or her. This "stay order" prohibits all creditors from taking any further steps to collect their debts from the debtor.

The court almost immediately sends a notice to each creditor listed by the debtor stating that a Petition for Bankruptcy under Chapter 7 of the Code has been filed and that a meeting of both the debtor and his or her creditors will be held at a designated time and place (usually in the office of the Trustee in Bankruptcy who has been assigned by the court). The notice also includes other information of importance to the creditors such as whether or not the creditors are to file proofs of claims with the court; the last date for filing an objection which may be either a complaint or protest against the debtor; and the impending action.

It is on immediate receipt of this notice of the filing for bankruptcy (or earlier if the creditor has been given advance notice by the debtor of his or her intent to file) that the creditor should take all actions available to him or her to overcome the Chapter 7 elimination of all debts (except certain tax payment obligations) and the debtor's obligation to repay them.

Things to Do

When notice of a Chapter 7 filing is received, the creditor should immediately do the following:

1. Conduct a current credit check of the debtor.

2. Check the current credit report against the credit report obtained when the debtor originally applied for the loan and against the list of debts on the debtor's loan application. If the new report lists obligations not stated on the original credit application, you have a potentially fraudulent application and ammunition to use in an effort to overturn the debtor's Chapter 7 application.

3. Review whatever additional information you requested of the debtor at the time he or she applied for his or her loan and determine whether or not all of the information supplied was truthful. If, for any reason, any of the information given on the original application now appears to have been false or if the debtor failed to give all of the information requested on the application, you again have potential grounds for claiming fraud on the part of the debtor and overthrowing the Chapter 7 application.

4. Contact the Bankruptcy Court or the debtor's attorney and request copies of the debtor's files. (You may have to pay the court a small fee for each copy made.) Obtain copies of the debtor's list of obligations, the list of his or her assets, and the statement of his or her financial affairs.

5. Compare all of the debtor's lists with the information you have gathered from the debtor's original application, any information your collection department may have gathered concerning the debtor and his or her obligations, and the review data you have collected. Again you are seeking out discrepancies which may give you grounds to claim fraud. Also, you may be aware of some assets the debtor has failed to include in the listing given to the court, or even of some debt (such as a loan at a company credit union) that is unlisted. Such a failure could also be a reason to overturn a Chapter 7 application.

6. If you have not been formally notified either by the debtor's attorney or by a notice from the court of the petition for bankruptcy, contact the debtor and request a reaffirmation of your loan. Inform the debtor that if he or she does not reaffirm before filing, you intend to attend the creditors' meeting and introduce whatever evidence you may have gathered of either fraud or omission in an effort to prevent the debtor from going into bankruptcy. If you have been formally notified of a filing or if you are aware that a debtor is being represented by an attorney, contact the attorney and ask for the same reaffirmation, telling the attorney of your intentions to go into the creditors' hearing and oppose the bankruptcy petition on the grounds of fraud or omission.

7. If you have no indication whatsoever of either fraud or deception in the application filed with you or in the list of debts or assets filed by the debtor, call the debtor's attorney and request a reaffirmation. Simply inform the attorney that if there is no reaffirmation of your debt you intend to participate in the creditors' meeting and to raise objections to the effort to obtain relief under Chapter 7. The knowledge that a creditor plans to fight the Chapter 7 petition (when the attorney has no advanced knowledge of the objections you will raise) will sometimes win a reaffirmation agreement for you because of the attorney's fear of a legitimate objection that may result in the Chapter 7 request being denied.

8. Most important! Attend the meeting of the creditors which has been scheduled and at which the debtor must appear (usually with his or her attorney) to be questioned by the Trustee in Bankruptcy, the creditors, and/or their attorneys. It is not unknown for a debtor or his or her attorney to fail to show at the hearing. And, if a creditor is there and the debtor does not appear, it is likely that the petition will be dismissed. You may find yourself the only creditor at the hearing, but, by being there you may be able to win a reaffirmation of your debt.

Following the creditors' meeting, the Trustee will make an effort to collect any nonexempt assets belonging to the debtor in the hope that enough money will be collected to repay some portion of the debtor's total outstanding unsecured debts.

After the Trustee has finished collecting the assets and the creditors have done whatever litigating they may elect to do, the court will hold a hearing and inform the debtor whether or not he or she will receive a discharge. If you have been successful in obtaining a reaffirmation agreement from the debtor, the court will cover it at this time.

Chapter 11 Bankruptcy

Chapter 11 of the Bankruptcy Code seldom applies to the individual debtor. It is most frequently used by the financially troubled business entity as an alternative to a Chapter 7 liquidation. There is no formal requirement that a debtor be conducting a business, however the provisions of Chapter 11 are designed to be unattractive to the debtor who is not. Chapter 11 contemplates rehabilitation through the consolidation and adjustment of debts and equity interest. It is similar to a Chapter 13 bankruptcy in that a plan is drawn up for repayment of outstanding debts from the future earnings of the business entity while relief is given by the court in terms of a stay prohibiting all creditors from taking any steps to collect their debts from the business. A Chapter 13 bankruptcy may be initiated by either the debtor or by one or more of the creditors. If it is initiated by a creditor it becomes an involuntary bankruptcy.

However, the court may assess a penalty against a creditor who files an involuntary bankruptcy under Chapter 11 if the debtor is successful in having the petition dismissed as being unwarranted.

As in the case of a Chapter 13 bankruptcy, under the Code, the Chapter 11 bankruptcy offers an alternative to liquidation. Rather than liquidating the debtor's assets and thus putting him or her out of business, the Chapter 11 procedure calls for a repayment plan of outstanding debts from contemplated future earnings according to a schedule prepared by the debtor, accepted by the creditors, and approved by the court.

Fighting Back

If a creditor receives notice of a Chapter 11 filing, he or she should proceed as suggested under the Chapter 7 discussion. If, on the other hand, a creditor has reason to believe that an individual borrower who is self-employed is in financial trouble and there is definite danger that an outstanding debt will not be repaid unless some action is taken, the creditor should explore the possibility of filing for the involuntary bankruptcy of the debtor under Chapter 11. If the creditor (or a group of creditors) initiates a Chapter 11 petition and it is denied, then the petitioner(s) may be required to pay any costs, attorneys' fees, and damages to the debtor. If it is found that a petition was filed in bad faith by the creditor(s), punitive damages may be awared also.

If the debtor has substantial assets which would pay off most or all of the outstanding debts if liquidated, a creditor may request the conversion of the Chapter 11 to a Chapter 7 bankruptcy. A conversion can be ordered if the court finds there is cause for it. Such cause includes no chance for a successful rehabilitation; a continuing eroding of the business; the unwillingness or inability to carry out or to develop a repayment plan; the denial of confirmation by the court; or the debtor's default on an approved repayment plan.

Chapter 13 Bankruptcy

Chapter 13 of the Bankruptcy Code offers the debtor an attractive alternative to the total liquidation of all of his or her nonexempt assets. Under Chapter 13, the debtor who has a regular source of income can make arrangements to repay his or her debts according to a schedule which he or she proposes to the court. Such repayment does not usually come from the liquidation of the debtor's property. Rather, some portion of the debtor's future income is designated to repay all or a portion of the outstanding debts within a set time frame. The debtor tenders a portion of her or his future earnings to the court-appointed trustee for payment to the creditors according to the approved repayment plan.

The Creditor Should Fight Back

Under a Chapter 13, secured debts continue to be honored and must be repaid by the debtor. However, the unsecured debts may be forgiven in whole or in part by the court depending on the debtor's plan. If the same steps as outlined under the Chapter 7 Bankruptcy section of this book are followed, it is possible that the creditor may be able to get his or her entire loan reaffirmed or else force the repayment of a larger portion of the debt than that proposed in the debtor's plan.

A Day At A Creditors' Meeting

The "Notice of a Meeting of Creditors" of a debtor who was filing for a Chapter 13 Bankruptcy was routed to the bank's senior personal loan officer. On receiving it, she took immediate action to determine if the bank could prevent the discharge.

She requested the customer's complete loan file. She sent a bank messenger to the Bankruptcy Court to obtain copies of the debtor's lists of assets and obligations and the statement of his financial affairs. She called the collection department and had them send to her whatever information they had gathered about the debtor during their collection activities. She ran through the bank's Customer Information File (C.I.F) to find out whether or not the debtor had any savings on deposit. The loan officer had her loan clerk pull a current credit report on the debtor. She then compared all the data she had gathered with the information given by the debtor on the original loan application and she contacted the savings department and put a freeze on the $100 she had found in a savings account belonging to the debtor. She also called the debtor's employer and reconfirmed his employment and his current salary.

What is the Current Value?

The loan officer confirmed that the borrower worked for a major company and she determined that he had been a member of its credit union because listed as a "paid up loan" on the original application was an auto loan from the company credit union. She contacted the credit union and asked if the customer was under a weekly payroll deduction program and if there was a current outstanding unsecured loan. She was answered in the affirmative.

The loan officer checked the current "guide to used car values" to determine the present worth of the debtor's automobile. And, she sent the bank's real estate appraiser out to do an appraisal on the debtor's house.

When she compared all the information she had pulled together with the debtor's original loan application and the information the debtor had given to the Bankruptcy Court, she found a number of omissions and discrepancies:

- The debtor had not listed either his savings account at his credit union or the fact that there was an outstanding loan at the credit union on which he was making preferential payments.

- The debtor had understated the worth of his automobile.

- The debtor had listed as the worth of his house the price he had purchased it for three years earlier.

- The bank's appraiser had determined from the registry of deeds that the debtor had transferred 50% of the ownership of his real estate into his girl friend's name two months before filing for bankruptcy.

With all these facts before her, the loan officer called the debtor's attorney and requested a reaffirmation of the bank's debt. She informed the attorney that she had information that could result in the bankruptcy petition being denied and that she intended to attend the meeting of creditors to present her findings. The attorney promised to talk it over with the debtor.

Later, against the attorney's advice, the debtor refused to reaffirm the bank's loan. So, the loan officer and the bank's attorney attended the meeting of creditors. It turned out that they were the only creditors in attendance so following a few questions from the United States Trustee in Bankruptcy, they were permitted to question the debtor. They quickly brought to light the hidden savings account at the credit union, the credit union loan and its preferential payments, the value of the automobile well in excess of the value stated by the petitioner, and, most devastating, the recent transfer of ownership of the debtor's real estate and its current value. Faced with these facts, the Trustee recommended to the debtor's attorney that he withdraw the petitioner's request for relief under Chapter 13. After a brief discussion with his client, the debtor's attorney requested that the application be withdrawn.

The loan officer had been successful in thwarting the customer's bankruptcy and in preventing a loss to the bank.

Appendix

Customer Rights Under the Financial Privacy Act

Fair Debt Collection Practices Act

CUSTOMER RIGHTS UNDER THE FINANCIAL PRIVACY ACT

Federal law protects the privacy of an individual's financial records. Before banks, credit unions, credit card companies, other financial institutions or creditors may give financial information about an individual to a federal agency, certain procedures must be followed.

Consent to Release of Financial Records

The individual may be asked to consent to make his or her financial records available to the government. He or she may withhold his or her consent, and his or her consent is not required as a condition of doing business with any financial institution.

Subpoena or Summons

Without the individual's consent, a federal agency that wants to see his or her financial records may do so ordinarily only by means of a lawful subpoena, summons, formal written request or search warrant for that purpose.

Generally, the federal agency must give the individual advance notice, explaining why the information is being sought and telling him or her how to object in court. The federal agency must also send him or her copies of court documents to be prepared by him or her with instructions for filling them out.

Exceptions

In some circumstances, a federal agency may obtain financial information about an individual without advance notice or his or her consent. For example, information may be released, when authorized by the Internal Revenue Code; when required by law to be reported; when there has been a possible violation of federal law; when required by a Federal loan program (however, the individual has the right to ask which agency(ies) obtained this loan information about him or her and when).

Transfer of Information

Generally, a federal agency must tell the individual if any records obtained from a financial institution are transferred to another federal agency.

Penalties

If a federal agency or financial institution violates the Financial Privacy Act, the individual may sue for damages or to seek compliance with the law. If the individual wins, he or she may be repaid attorney's fees and costs.

Additional Information

If the individual has any questions about his or her rights under this law, or about how to consent to release of his or her financial records, please call (*phone number of lender's office that answers customer privacy questions.*)

FAIR DEBT COLLECTION PRACTICES ACT

Background

The Fair Debt Collection Practices Act (the Act), 15 USC § 1692 *et seq.*, was signed into law on September 20, 1977, as Title VIII of the Consumer Credit Protection Act. The effective date of the Act is March 20, 1978. It is designed to eliminate abusive and deceptive debt collection practices and to insure that reputable debt collectors are not competitively disadvantaged.

Coverage

Not all persons or businesses who collect debts are covered by the Act. The Act defines "debt collector" as any person who regularly collects or attempts to collect, directly or indirectly, consumer debts asserted to be owed to another person. Consumer debt is debt incurred by an individual primarily for personal, family, or household purposes. Debts incurred for business or agricultural purposes are not covered.

A lender will *not* be a debt collector subject to the Act when it:

- Collects debts due another only in isolated instances.

- Collects, in the lender's own name, debts owed to the lender.

- Collects a debt which it originated.

- Collects a debt not in default when obtained.

- Collects a debt obtained as security for a commercial credit transaction involving the lender.

- Collects a debt incidental to a bona fide fiduciary relationship or escrow arrangement.

- Collects a debt for another person to whom it is related by common ownership or corporate control, as long as it does so *only* for those persons to whom it is so related. *However*, if the lender regularly collects defaulted debts owed a non-affiliate person, the lender will become a debt collector for those defaulted debts as well as for defaulted debts of affiliated entities, but not for its own debts.

Others who are *not* covered by the Act are:

- An officer or employee of the lending institution when collecting, in the lender's name, debts owed to the lender.
- Attorneys-at-law collecting debts on behalf of and in the name of the lender.
- Legal process servers.

Requirements

The Act requires debt collectors:

- To cease further communication with a consumer upon written request, except to advise the consumer that the debt collector's further efforts are being terminated, or to notify the consumer that specified remedies may or will be invoked.
- To apply payments in accordance with the consumer's instructions.
- To notify the consumer in writing, if the following information is not provided at initial contact, within five days of initial contact, of the amount of the debt and the name of the creditor, and to advise the consumer of the debt collector's duty to verify the debt if it is disputed. If the consumer disputes the debt within 30 days, the debt collector must stop collection efforts until verification is sent to the consumer.

Prohibitions

The Act prohibits:

- *Abuse and Harassment* - Threatening violence or using profane language in the collection of a debt.
- *False and Misleading Representation* - Threatening to communicate false credit information, or giving a false impression that collection documents represent legal process.
- *Unfair Practices* - Misusing postdated checks, or communicating by postcard.

  Among the activities specifically prohibited by the Act are the following:

- With limited exceptions, contact with third parties, including employers, except to obtain information concerning the consumer's location.
- Communication with the consumer at place of employment if there is reason to believe that the employer prohibits such communications.

- Contact with a consumer at any unusual time or place, unless agreed to by the consumer.

- Bringing a debt collection action in a jurisdiction other than those permitted by the Act.

Civil Liability

Private civil action must be brought within one year from the date of the violation. In an individual action, the debt collector is liable for actual damages plus punitive damages of up to $1,000. In a class action, the debt collector is liable for actual damages, as well as punitive damages up t $1,000 for each named plaintiff and the lesser of 1% of net worth or $500,000 for all other class members.

Administrative Enforcement

Bank regulatory agencies are responsible for enforcing the Act under § 8 of the Federal Deposit Insurance Act. This means that bank regulators may use their authority under §8 to issue cease and desist orders which may include provisions requiring affirmative action to correct conditions resulting from violations. No regulations can be issued by any regulator, although the Federal Trade Commission has the authority to issue advisory opinions.

Glossary

Acceleration   The ability of the creditor to call for immediate payment of an entire debt in the event of certain specified occurrences such as the failure of the borrower to make payments on dates due.

Actual Interest   The amount of interest in exact dollars and cents you pay on a debt over the life of a loan.

Add-on Contract   A credit sales contract which gives the seller title to *all* items purchased by the debtor over a period of time until all payments due for all merchandise are made in full, even if sufficient payments have been made to pay off some of the items purchased.

Adequate Notice   The printed notice the lender is legally required to give to the borrower stating the exact terms of either a consumer loan or an installment purchase prior to the consumer becoming obligated for a debt.

Amortization   To repay a debt over an extended period of time rather than having it come due in one large lump sum after a relatively short period of time.

Amount Financed   The actual amount of credit or of a loan which the borrower receives and on which a finance charge or interest must be paid.

Annual Percentage Rate (A.P.R.)   The measure of the actual cost of credit assessed annually against the amount borrowed.

Automatic Line of Credit   A loan limit established in advance and extended to a borrower which permits him or her to automatically borrow at some future date to the extent of the credit line.

Balance   The remaining amount still due to be paid on a loan.

Balloon Contract   A loan agreement that requires a final payment much greater than the regular periodic payments made up to that point.

Bank Credit Card   A multiple credit card issued by a bank to its customers which permits the purchase of goods and services or the borrowing of cash from a number of retailers.

Bankruptcy   The insolvency of an individual by petition to a court, which in turn administers and divides the debtor's available property among his or her creditors.

Billing Cycle   The regular interval between the payment-due dates of a loan, usually every 30 days or monthly; or the frequency of payments (monthly, quarterly, semi-annually, or seasonally) during a 12-month period.

Billing Error   A mistake made by the lender on the billing statement sent to the debtor. Regardless of whether or not a disputed item is actually a mistake, according to law the creditor must deal with it as a billing error if the debtor complains.

Binder   In conjunction with a sales contract, an item of value (usually cash) given to the seller by the buyer as an indication of the buyer's good faith intent to carry out the terms of the purchase agreement.

Borrower   An individual who borrows money or makes a purchase on time. Also known as the "debtor."

Card Holder   The individual to whom a credit card or debit card is either issued or who assumes another's obligations for card use.

Carrying Charges   A sum greater than the purchase price or the amount borrowed which the debtor agrees to pay to the lender for the privilege of repaying the debt over a period of time.

Charge Account   An account usually established with a retail merchant which permits an individual to make purchases on credit rather than for cash and to pay for such purchases at a later date.

Charge Off   What happens to an unpaid debt when the creditor determines that it is uncollectible from the debtor for whatever reason. When such a debt no longer becomes a "receivable" or ceases to be considered an asset of the creditor, it is "charged off" and removed from the creditor's books.

Closed-End Loan   A loan in which the amount to be financed, the total amount due, the number of payments to be made, and the payment due dates are established and accepted in advance of the actual loan transaction.

Closing Costs   Additional costs (other than finance charges) levied against a loan at the time the loan is executed. Such costs may include legal costs, insurance costs, and credit investigation charges.

Closing Date   The day on which monthly statements for credit payments and purchases are calculated. Information received after that day of either payments or purchases, regardless of when contracted, will appear on future statements.

Collateral   Assets pledged by a borrower to a lender as security for a loan.

Comaker/Cosigner   A second individual who, together with the original borrower, signs a note or a purchase contract and assumes equal liability for its repayment.

Confession of Judgment   A clause in a note by which the borrower waives all legal rights in the event he or she misses a single payment on his or her installment loan.

Conditional Sales Contract *or* Third Party Paper   One that gives the creditor the legal right to repossess goods sold to the debtor in the event of failure to make payments when due.

Consumer   Defined by law as a person who uses goods or services for personal, family, or household purposes, as distinguished from a business purchaser.

Consumer Credit   Credit extended to an individual for personal, family, or household purposes only.

Consumer Reporting Agency   A private agency, usually a credit bureau, that collects, maintains, and distributes information about the credit worthiness of individuals.

Credit   Time given by a lender to a borrower to repay money borrowed or for goods purchased on trust.

Credit Card   One of an estimated 400 million cards in use in the United States by both businesses and consumers to make purchases on credit or to borrow cash.

Credit Insurance   Life and/or accident-health insurance made available by some creditors which pays a loan in the event of a debtor's disability or death.

Credit Rating   The evaluation of an individual's credit worthiness based on his or her past history of borrowing, repaying, and employment.

Credit Sales Disclosure   A legally-required form which details a lender's terms and conditions and which must be given to a borrower before he or she completes a credit transaction.

Creditor   An individual or company that extends credit and to whom payment is due.

Dealer Financing   A situation where the seller (dealer) serves as a middleman who initiates the procedure for the bank or finance company which actually lends the money for the purchase. The dealer serves as a financing agent providing the purchaser with the necessary papers and then processing them through to the lender.

Debit Card   A card used by an individual to obtain cash or to pay for a purchase. The debit card permits the bank or merchant to immediately remove the exact amount of the transaction from the individual's savings or checking account. If sufficient funds are not in the account to cover the transaction, the debit card could become a debit/credit card and create an overdraft loan.

Debt Consolidation   An arrangement whereby a lender agrees to make one large loan to a debtor to pay off a number of smaller loans. Because the larger loan is spread out over a long period of time and requires only regular single monthly payments, the debtor usually is better able to meet his or her payments.

Debt Pooling   *See* Debt Consolidation.

Default   The failure to pay a debt when due or to live up to the terms and conditions of a contract.

Deficiency Judgment   The legal permission given to the creditor by a clause in the loan contract which assigns a security interest to the creditor permitting him or her to take possession of specified collateral in the event of default.

Delayed Payment   Usually a promotional plan extended to a debtor by a creditor whereby permission is given to delay making a regularly due payment for one or two months or more, usually at holiday times. Thus: "Buy now for Christmas. First payment not due until February."

Delinquency   A loan account on which payment is past due.

Deposit   A down payment made at the time of a purchase. Some loans may be granted only if a minimum deposit is first made to the creditor.

Depreciation   The decrease in value due to age and/or use of merchandise which reduces the worth of security purchased through a secured loan.

Discounted Loan   A loan sold to a third party by the original lender for less than the face amount of the loan contract. This is the usual way a bank credit card purchase is made. The merchant agrees to take a percentage discount off the amount of the purchase in return for the bank paying the merchant immediately in cash or credit. The bank then collects the entire amount of the original purchase from the debtor.

Down Payment   Money paid by the purchaser at the time the decision to buy is made. The down payment (or deposit) guarantees that the merchandise will be held until payment in full is made at a future date either through installment payments directly to the seller or payment in full to the seller by a third party such as a bank with whom the purchaser has made arrangements for a secured loan.

Education Loan   A special loan to pay tuition and other educational expenses at colleges or private schools. Such loans may be granted by the federal or state government or by the school itself. These are usually at very low interest rates and are not repayable until the student has left the school.

Endorser   An individual who signs a loan contract and assumes responsibility for repayment if the original maker defaults. *See*: Comaker/Cosigner.

Equal Credit Opportunity Act (E.C.O.A.)   A 1975 federal law which bars discrimination in lending for reasons of sex, marital status, race, color, religion, national origin, age, or income.

Equity   That portion of ownership vested to the borrower into property purchased on credit as payments on the loan are made. Thus, if 50% of the purchase price of the property is repaid, the debtor has 50% equity.

Fair Credit Billing Act   An amendment to the Truth-In-Lending Act which enables debtors to dispute billings and withhold payments until questions are resolved without adversely affecting credit ratings or incurring loan penalties.

Fair Credit Reporting Act (FCRA)   Gives consumers the right to be told when a credit report has been used against him or her, the right to know the content of the report, and the right to correct the file if in error.

Finance Charge   The cost of credit for a loan. The Federal Truth-In-Lending Act requires that lenders detail all finance charges levied against a loan or credit purchase.

Finance Company   A private lending company that provides money or credit to individuals for the purchase of goods or services through installment loan contracts.

Garnishment   A court order requiring an employer to withhold part of an employee's compensation and pay it to one of the employee's creditors.

Holder in Due Course   The third-party purchaser of a credit or loan contract. *See*: Discounted Loan.

Home Improvement Loan   A loan granted solely to a home owner for the express purpose of remodelling or renovating a dwelling place. It is calculated like any other personal loan except that it is usually larger in total amount granted and extends over a longer period of time.

Installment Loan   A loan or credit purchase that is repaid in regularly scheduled amounts over a specified period of time.

Insurance on Loans   *See*: Credit Insurance.

Interest   The amount of money the debtor pays to the creditor for the use of the borrowed money or extended credit.

Interest, Compound   Interest paid on interest.

Interest, Simple   The amount of interest paid for the use of money for one year on a per diem basis.

Irregular   The debtor who establishes a pattern of irregular but eventual repayment by skipping payments, paying in larger amounts then smaller amounts than required, or making partial payments.

Judgment   A court ruling for a specific amount to be repaid on a delinquent loan by a debtor.

Juice   The exorbitant interest rate charged by a loan shark to a borrower.

Kicker   Additional charges other than interest levied against the borrower by the lender for the privilege of granting the loan or extending the credit. Usually a "service or handling fee" for the work involved in creating the credit documentation.

Lease Agreement   A contract that permits the use of a product for a period of time in exchange for periodic payments.

Leverage   The use of borrowed funds to increase the earning power of one's own funds. For example: an individual buys a house for $100,000 using $10,000 of his or her own money and a $90,000 bank mortgage. He or she then sells the house for $150,000. He or she has "leveraged" the original $10,000 investment into a profit of $50,000.

Lien   A creditor's claim against a debtor's property to recover debt payments owed.

Loan Companies   *See*: Finance Company

Loans   An advance of money or credit by a lender with the expectation of repayment in the future.

Loans, Secured   Loans with the value insured by the pledge of property which becomes the property of the lender in the event of default.

Loan, Unsecured   Loan extended solely on the basis of the borrower's credit worthiness and promise to repay.

Maturity Date   The date on which a final payment is due on a loan.

Mortgage   A loan granted to purchase valuable property in which the property itself is pledged as collateral to secure the loan.

Mouse-House   In conjunction with the financing of an automobile through a car dealer, the dealer has the buyer sign a separate chattel loan with a finance company. The car-buyer seldom knows he or she has been "mouse-housed" until he or she begins receiving monthly bills from the finance company.

Ninety-Day Charge Plans   A credit purchase plan usually offered by a department store or retail merchant who permits a customer to repay a credit purchase in three monthly payments without carrying charges or interest.

Note, Promissory   A written promise to repay a loan.

Oil Company Cards   A credit card issued by an oil company for the purchase of goods and services at the oil company's retail outlets and sometimes elsewhere.

Open-End Credit   An agreement with a lender whereby the borrower is permitted to make a number of purchases or to obtain a number of cash advances up to a maximum limit established at the time the credit agreement was executed.

Option to Buy   In conjunction with a lease permission is given to purchase the leased item at a future time and at a stated price. *See*: Lease Agreement.

Outstanding Debt   The exact amount of money still owed to the lender at any specific time.

Passbook Loan   A loan against the savings in a passbook savings account. The passbook is usually held by the lender as collateral.

Point   One percent of the loan amount especially with a mortgage. *See*: Kicker.

Prepayment Penalty   A charge levied against the borrower when the loan is repaid in full in advance of the maturity date.

Prepayment Privilege   A guarantee that there will be no penalty charge for early repayment of a loan.

Prime Rate   The most favorable interest rate that banks charge their best business customers.

Rebate   The return to a debtor of a portion of the discount or add-on interest amount owed to the creditor.

Replevin   *See*: Repossession

Repossession   The recovery of merchandise purchased through a secured loan by the lender when the borrower fails to meet the terms of the loan contract. *See*: Conditional Sales Contract.

Rescission, Right of   The right of a borrower to cancel a contract to purchase goods or services or to borrow money.

Revolving Credit   A charge account by which a borrower may purchase items up to a maximum dollar value limit and, as repayment is made, can make additional purchases again up to the established limit.

Secured Loan   *See*: Loan, Secured

Service Charge   The percentage charged to a retail merchant by a credit card issuer for purchasing the sales contract created through the use of a credit card.

Simple Annual Interest   *See*: Interest, Simple.

Student Loan   *See*: Education Loan.

T and E Cards.   Travel and entertainment cards for credit purchases usually at restaurants and airlines. Privately issued by such companies as American Express and Diners Club.

Terms   The conditions agreed to in a loan or credit contract.

True Interest   The rate (percentage of the fixed principal amount borrowed) charged for the use of that money for one full year on a per diem basis. *See*: Interest, Simple.

Truth-In-Lending   The Consumer Credit Protection Act of 1969. A Federal Law that applies to practically all consumer credit transactions under $25,000.

Unsecured Loan   *See*: Loan, Unsecured.

Usury Laws   State and federal laws that prohibit charging an excessive rate of interest.

Vacation Loans   Consumer installment loans granted for the purpose of taking a vacation. Also known as a "luxury loan."

Wage Garnishment   *See*: Garnishment.

Index